How to Write a Novel

A Guide With Tips Collected on My Own Writing

(How to Write Fiction & Non Fiction Books and Build Your Author Platform)

Aaron Mohr

Published By **John Kembrey**

Aaron Mohr

All Rights Reserved

How to Write a Novel: A Guide With Tips Collected on My Own Writing (How to Write Fiction & Non Fiction Books and Build Your Author Platform)

ISBN 978-0-9952939-9-1

No part of this guidebook shall be reproduced in any form without permission in writing from the publisher except in the case of brief quotations embodied in critical articles or reviews.

Legal & Disclaimer

The information contained in this book is not designed to replace or take the place of any form of medicine or professional medical advice. The information in this book has been provided for educational & entertainment purposes only.

The information contained in this book has been compiled from sources deemed reliable, and it is accurate to the best of the Author's knowledge; however, the Author cannot guarantee its accuracy and validity and cannot be held liable for any errors or omissions. Changes are periodically made to this book. You must consult your doctor or get professional medical advice before using any of the suggested remedies, techniques, or information in this book.

Upon using the information contained in this book, you agree to hold harmless the Author from and against any damages, costs, and expenses, including any legal fees potentially resulting from the application of any of the information provided by this guide. This disclaimer applies to any damages or injury caused by the use and application, whether directly or indirectly, of any advice or information presented, whether for breach of contract, tort, negligence, personal injury, criminal intent, or under any other cause of action.

You agree to accept all risks of using the information presented inside this book. You need to consult a professional medical practitioner in order to ensure you are both able and healthy enough to participate in this program.

Table Of Contents

Chapter 1: The International Of Writing ... 1

Chapter 2: The Importance Of Originality 13

Chapter 3: Creating Memorable Characters 21

Chapter 4: Discovering Your Writing Fashion 35

Chapter 5: The Infamous Writer's Block Syndrome 46

Chapter 6: Beta Readers To Acquire Treasured Remarks 59

Chapter 7: Handling Descriptions And Information 69

Chapter 8: The Ebook Of Your Novel 76

Chapter 9: Focus On Self-Publishing To Launch 80

Chapter 10: Advertising And Marketing .. 87

Chapter 11: How To Enhance Your Competencies Over The Years 98

Chapter 12: Story Vs. Plot 107

Chapter 13: The Hook 120

Chapter 14: The Inciting Incident 133

Chapter 15: Three Act Structure 142

Chapter 16: Description 160

Chapter 17: Show, Don't Tell 167

Chapter 18: Dialogue 176

Chapter 1: The International Of Writing

I invite you to discover the mysterious and often fantastical global of writing by using the usage of studying the worrying situations authors face and the numerous possibilities that watch for them. Writing is each an art work and a annoying area. For the ones humans who've chosen this creative route, we're pushed via the ardour to inform testimonies and percentage our ideas with the arena. However, it is critical to recognize that writing is a adventure packed with obstacles, wherein every creator want to confront unique demanding situations.

One of the initial demanding situations writers frequently face is self-doubt. When embarking on the writing of a completely unique, it isn't uncommon to question whether or not or not our story is properly worth telling, if our writing style measures up, and if we're capable of captivate readers. This feel of uncertainty may be paralyzing, however it is critical to consider that every author, even the maximum famous ones, has felt this sooner or later. The key's to persevere and recall why we write within the first area.

Another huge undertaking is time control. For many authors, writing is a ardour that need to coexist with other obligations together with paintings, own family, and social obligations. Finding time to sit down and write often may be difficult; however it's far essential to development in a single's literary assignment. Creating a devoted writing schedule and sticking to it as loads as viable is useful.

In addition to the ones personal stressful situations, the area of publishing also provides unique hurdles. Finding a conventional publishing house to put up a novel can be a prolonged and difficult manner, regularly marked with the aid of way of way of commonplace rejections. Publishing homes achieve masses of manuscripts every year, and handiest a fragment of them are famous for e-book. Therefore, patience and perseverance are essential in this project.

Fortunately, self-publishing has become an an increasing number of well-known option for authors. Through self-publishing systems like Amazon Kindle Direct Publishing (KDP), authors have the opportunity to independently placed up their novels. This opens up new possibilities for writers to show off their artwork to the general public without going via the traditional publishing technique.

The creation of the Internet and social media has additionally created new possibilities for authors. Blogs, author net net sites, story-sharing structures, and social networks permit writers to connect right now with their goal market and assemble a loyal fan base. Self-promoting and developing an internet presence have grow to be crucial abilities for authors who need to face out in this tremendous literary global.

Another element of the writing international is the range of literary genres. Each fashion offers its very very personal demanding situations and possibilities. Some authors favor to delve into the fantastical imagination, while others sense at domestic in the mysterious surroundings of crime fiction. Regardless of the chosen style, it is important to apprehend the expectations and codes precise to each form of narrative whilst infusing it with one's non-public contact.

Finally, it is essential to don't forget that writing is mainly an act of creativity and private expression. Even even though demanding conditions can also furthermore appear daunting, every obstacle overcome is an possibility to expand as a writer. Opportunities are countless, and each web web page you write brings you in the direction of know-how your literary goals.

How to discover perception

The writing of a completely unique often starts offevolved with the emergence of a simple idea. But a manner to have that concept, that supply of concept as a manner to offer start to a captivating story? We will find out considered one of a kind assets of contemporary mind to help you generate unique and exciting requirements in your novel.

1. Observing the world around us: normal existence is complete of fascinating memories. Observe human beings, places, and sports activities round you. Interactions in a café, conversations overheard in a park, or perhaps visits to a museum can be an limitless supply of idea. Keep an assertion magazine, be aware the records that strike you, and allow your imagination capture the ones moments to convert them into novelistic plots.

2. Reading widely and diversely: analyzing is an infinite supply of idea for any author. Explore special literary genres, from traditional to contemporary, from fiction to non-fiction. Reading various works broadens your angle and permits you to find out new thoughts and perspectives. You may also

moreover even discover concept in a character, a scene, or a line of dialogue in a e-book.

three. Questions and "what if": pose provocative questions to yourself and allow your imagination run wild. "what if" is a paranormal phrase for writers trying to find notion. What if a time tourist landed in the past and changed the route of history[1] ? What if a mysterious letter determined a well-guarded secret? The possibilities are endless, so do now not restrict your creativeness.

4. Research: research additionally can be a supply of innovative thoughts. Explore historical records, overseas cultures, scientific phenomena, and discover particular angles to take benefit of for your novel. Even in fiction, a strong know-how base can lend credibility on your story and boom it with exciting statistics.

five. Dreams and the unconscious: our goals can be gateways to a worldwide of imagination. Keep a dream magazine through way of using your bed and jot down your goals as speedy as you wake up. They can be a goldmine for enigmatic scenes or captivating hassle subjects. The subconscious is a powerful supply of idea, so do now not hesitate to discover your internal most thoughts.

6. Music, art, and high-quality varieties of innovative expression: song, paintings, movies, and exceptional types of paintings can evoke emotions and pics to your mind. Use them as a deliver of idea to create atmospheres, moods, or subjects to your novel. Let yourself be over excited by way of the use of melodies and colours to nourish your creativity.

7. Travel and opinions: exploring new locations and having new tales can develop your worldview and provide unique factors to include in your novel. Whether it's miles a journey remote places or a clean getaway to a nearby town, the enjoy of recent places and cultures can be a rich deliver of perception.

8. Memories and emotions: your very own reminiscences and feelings may be an intimate supply of idea. Drawing from your lived reviews will will let you infuse your novel with authenticity and emotion. You can create characters who go through comparable trials to yours or use robust feelings to shape the surroundings of your story.

Finding concept is a personal and unique approach for each creator. Don't be discouraged if the ideal concept could not proper away floor. Keep an open mind, live curious, and do now not underestimate the strength of your imagination.

Choosing a literary style

The preference of literary fashion is a essential step in the writing of a novel. Each style offers particular traits and conventions that affect the tone, fashion, and target market of your tale. Let's discover superb literary genres. This will assist you discover the simplest that amazing suits your idea and innovative vision.

1. General fiction: desired fiction is a massive style that encompasses a mess of topics and topics. If you have a tale to tell with out limiting your self to precise conventions, excellent fiction may be your preference. It gives the liberty to find out complex characters and human dilemmas while challenge a good sized target market.

2. Science fiction: technological expertise fiction is a fashion that pushes the boundaries of creativeness. If you're attracted to futuristic worlds, advanced technology, location tour, or philosophical questions about the future of humanity, technology fiction is for you. This fashion lets in you to find out medical, social, or political requirements on the equal time as developing particular universes.

three. Fantasy: delusion is a style that draws from myths, legends, and the imaginary. If you are interested in magical worlds, incredible creatures, epic quests, and the warfare amongst precise and evil, fantasy is the first-class desire. This style gives countless innovative freedom, in which you could create specific universes and suggestions in your narrative.

four. Mystery and mystery: thriller and thriller are genres that captivate readers with puzzles, complex plots, and plot twists. If you enjoy weaving mysteries, developing thrilling characters, and maintaining your readers on area till the prevent, this fashion lets in you to play with expectancies and revelations.

five. Romance: romance is a fashion that explores human emotions, romantic relationships, and the stressful situations characters face to discover love. If you're obsessed with love tales, easy moments, and topics of the coronary heart, romance offers an opportunity to awaken readers' feelings.

6. Crime and noir: crime and noir are genres that concentrate on crook investigations, detectives, and mysteries to clear up. If you are drawn to the investigative aspect and hassle-solving, those genres can be fertile

floor for growing fascinating plots and captivating characters.

7. Contemporary literature: cutting-edge literature is a style that addresses current-day-day problems and general topics realistically. If you are inquisitive about reminiscences of regular existence, human relationships, and the challenges of modern-day-day society, modern-day literature offers an opportunity for pondered photo and emotional reference to readers.

eight. Fantasy and paranormal: fantasy and paranormal are genres that introduce supernatural factors into a realistic global. If you're interested in unusual phenomena, supernatural powers, or encounters with the beyond, those genres allow you to discover mystery and the occult.

Choosing the literary fashion that amazing fits your concept requires notion and exploration. Take the time to have a observe outstanding genres, examine iconic works from every elegance, and concentrate on your revolutionary instincts. You also can test through manner of writing essays in a single in each of a type genres to look which one evokes you the most.

Remember that you aren't constrained to a single style. Many authors skillfully mixture particular genres to create precise stories. The secret's to discover the style that resonates together together with your imaginative and prescient and allows you to tell your tale in the most real way feasible.

Chapter 2: The Importance Of Originality

In a international wherein lots of novels are posted every three hundred and sixty five days, fame out as a author can also appear to be an insurmountable project. However, there's a critical excellent that will let you shine amongst special authors: originality. We will find out the importance of originality in writing and the manner to domesticate your unique voice to captivate your readers.

1. Think out of doors the sector: originality lies within the capacity to think out of doors the field and discover uncharted territories. Don't be afraid to test with new mind, take modern dangers, and mission style conventions. Readers are looking for clean and surprising stories that transport them into the unknown.

2. Find your author's voice: each creator has a totally precise voice of their very non-public. This is what makes your art work particular and incredible. Don't attempting to find to mimic distinctive a fulfillment writers; as an

opportunity, cultivate your personal fashion. Be real to your writing and allow your character shine through your phrases.

3. Explore popular troubles in an specific way: favored topics along with love, loss, courage, and desire have been tackled frequently in literature. To stand out, are looking for for to find out them in an authentic and personal way. Find a very specific mind-set to address the ones concern subjects or combine them unexpectedly to create a trendy mind-set.

4. Create memorable characters: characters are the soul of any tale. To be precise, expand complicated characters with deep motivations and internal conflicts. Avoid stereotypes and supply your characters specific tendencies with a view to make them unforgettable on your readers.

five. Avoid clichés: clichés are worn-out and predictable factors that can weaken your story. Avoid conditions, dialogues, and plot twists which may be too familiar. Look for specific techniques to treatment issues and enhance your plot.

6. Be ambitious: originality calls for boldness. Don't be timid for your writing. Dare to discover controversial difficulty topics, ambiguous characters, or surprising resolutions. Readers are inquisitive about authors who dare to push the bounds of creativity.

7. Seek proposal without copying: belief can come from numerous property, but it's important to distinguish notion from copying. If you're inspired through the paintings of different authors, take it as a catalyst to nurture your very very own creativity, however do not plagiarize their art work. Find the way to combine your precise ideas into your narrative.

eight. Solicit top notch comments: to make certain that your originality resonates with readers, do not hesitate to are searching for positive feedback from beta readers or writing agencies. Feedback will allow you to refine your tale and ensure that your originality is certainly perceived by means of your goal marketplace.

Ultimately, originality is the critical thing to reputation out in a competitive marketplace. Don't are looking for to delight everybody; as an possibility, recognition on the actual expression of your voice as a author. Your originality is your most powerful asset to draw passionate readers and create a long-lasting connection with them.

The foundation of your narrative is primarily based at the improvement of your form

In writing a novel, the shape is the spine of your tale. A accurate form gives your narrative with coherence, fluidity, and narrative power. We will discover the basics of storytelling and manual you grade by grade to construct a stable form to be able to captivate your readers.

1. The triggering detail: the whole thing begins with the triggering element, the event

or situation that gadgets the plot of your novel in motion. It's the instant while everything adjustments on your protagonist, and he or she or he's propelled proper right into a quest or struggle that lets in you to force the story.

2. Narrative arc: the narrative arc is the development of the story from starting to give up. It follows the trajectory of the protagonist as he faces annoying conditions, evolves emotionally, and makes picks that bring him in the direction of resolving the plot. The narrative arc need to be normal and well-developed to preserve the readers' interest.

three. Turning factors: turning factors are key moments within the tale wherein the plot takes a cutting-edge flip or great revelations are made. These moments are crucial to retaining suspense and retaining readers engaged. Turning elements can consist of revelations approximately characters, surprising twists, or pastime-converting events.

four. Build-up of anxiety: the assemble-up of tension is the approach of growing dramatic anxiety in the end of the narrative. This includes introducing escalating limitations and conflicts for the protagonist, finding out him and pushing him to his limits. The better the anxiety, the extra captivated readers might be via using your story.

five. Climax: the climax is the very great point of the plot, the immediate of greatest anxiety and warfare. It's in which the opposing forces war decisively, and the stakes are at their maximum. The climax is the important component 2d while the protagonist faces his closing project and have to make a critical desire.

6. Resolution: the choice is the realization of the story wherein narrative threads come collectively, and most important questions discover their solutions. It's the on the spot at the same time as the results of the

protagonist's movements are observed out, and characters evolve or discover choice to their narrative arcs.

7. Subplots: further to the precept plot, subplots upload intensity and complexity in your novel. They allow for in addition man or woman improvement, exploration of secondary subjects, and weaving connections among exceptional elements of the story.

8. Consistency and stability: a extraordinary narrative form calls for consistency and stability. Ensure that every scene and event contributes to the development of the plot and the improvement of characters. Avoid inconsistencies or vain detours that might distract readers from the essence of your tale.

nine. Character development: characters are the pillars of your novel. Make positive to growth them thoroughly and continually in a few unspecified time within the future of the tale. Their motivations, feelings, and narrative arcs need to be in element related to the primary plot.

10. The significance of the begin and the give up: the begin of your novel is important to hooking readers' interest from the number one pages. It have to gift the triggering detail, introduce the protagonist, and set the tone for the tale. The surrender, instead, must provide a satisfying choice on the identical time as leaving a protracted-lasting influence on readers.

By building a strong form on your novel, you create a framework that allows you to guide your writing and supply your narrative a powerful effect. Take the time to devise your form, however furthermore be open to the evolution of your story in the direction of the writing manner. A well-concept-out shape will assist you live on course whilst allowing you the freedom to discover and create.

Chapter 3: Creating Memorable Characters

The characters are the hearts and souls of your novel. Well-advanced and incredible characters are critical to captivate your readers and draw them into your tale. We will find out the stairs to create actual and charming characters so that you can stay engraved within the minds of your readers.

1. Character complexity: people are complicated, with motivations, desires, fears, and contradictions. Your characters have to replicate this complexity to seem practical. Give them first-rate trends, functions, and flaws, in addition to inner motivations that cause them to precise.

2. Character profile: to higher understand your characters, create an intensive individual profile. Include information along with their bodily look, historical beyond, goals, beliefs, fears, and desires. The extra you apprehend approximately your characters, the much less

difficult it's going to likely be to growth them continuously for the duration of the story.

3. Character arcs: everyone ought to have their very own character arc, an emotional and mental evolution in the path of the story. Determine wherein they begin and quit their adventure, in addition to the important thing steps that cause them to evolve. The person arc need to be related to the principle plot, reinforcing the brotherly love of your novel.

four. Motivations and conflicts: person motivations pressure the tale. What compels them to behave? What are their goals and dreams? Additionally, internal and outside conflicts are critical to feature intensity for your characters and confront them with demanding situations that cause growth.

5. Character relationships: interactions amongst characters are an crucial trouble of your narrative. Create complex and nuanced relationships between them. Friendships, love, opposition, or own family ties deliver interesting dynamics to the story. Conflicts

and alliances among characters additionally may be a further deliver of intrigue.

6. Antiheroes and ambiguous characters: characters do now not have to be best. Antiheroes, human beings with darkish traits or marked flaws, may be clearly as fascinating as conventional heroes. Ambiguous characters, whose motivations are not usually clean, upload layers of mystery and complexity to the tale.

7. Character evolution thru activities: characters ought to be transformed via the sports activities of the tale. How do the recollections they go through change them? How does it have an effect on their relationships and alternatives? Character evolution is a powerful manner to preserve readers' interest inside the course of the radical.

eight. Dialogue and person voice: speak is an essential manner of bringing your characters to lifestyles. Ensure that their way of speakme is consistent with their individual and social context. Each character have to have a completely unique voice that displays their character and feelings.

nine. Reader empathy: for readers to connect with your characters, they need to revel in empathy towards them. Show their vulnerabilities, doubts, and feelings. The extra readers can pick out with the characters, the more emotionally invested they may be inside the story.

10. Secondary characters: neglecting secondary characters may be a mistake. They can upload intensity in your fictional world and assist increase the primary characters. Give them interest and make certain they serve a big cause in the tale.

Creating memorable characters is a touchy however profitable technique. Take the time to discover them in-depth, apprehend their motivations and emotions, and supply them rich individual arcs. Well-built characters will enhance your narrative and captivate your readers.

The hero's journey

The hero's adventure is a effective and timeless narrative sample located in plenty of a hit recollections, as Joseph Campbell examined in his essay titled 'The Hero with 1000 faces.' It follows the protagonist, the hero, through a chain of trials and changes that reason the selection of the plot. We will discover the key elements of the hero's adventure narrative arc and the way to use them to create a compelling story.

1. The name to journey: it all starts offevolved offevolved with the decision to journey, the event or project that activates the hero to go away their normal global and embark on a quest. This call can be a hazard, an opportunity, or an internal desire that awakens the need for exchange.

2. The refusal of the decision: initially, the hero may be reluctant to reply the decision to journey. They can be scared of the unknown or have doubts approximately their functionality to face the undertaking. This

refusal is a large step that highlights the protagonist's internal conflict.

3. Meeting the mentor: alongside the manner, the hero encounters a mentor, a manual, or an pleasant friend who permits conquer doubts and acquire new capabilities. The mentor plays a crucial function in inspiring and guiding the hero on their quest.

4. Crossing the brink: crossing the brink marks the instant at the identical time because the hero completely leaves their normal global to enter the place of journey. It is a tremendous sized transitional moment in which they need to confront the unknown and the disturbing situations that watch for.

five. Trials and allies: at some point of their journey, the hero faces trials and barriers that ought to be overcome to gain their cause. They may also additionally furthermore come across allies who help them of their quest and provide critical resource.

6. Approaching the innermost cave: the innermost cave represents the coronary coronary coronary heart of darkness, the place in which the hero confronts the nice project or revelation. It is a moment of tension and transformation in which they need to stand their private fears.

7. The climax: the climax is the prevent end result of the hero's journey, the instantaneous once they face their final undertaking. It is a second of dramatic intensity in which the stakes are maximum, and they need to make a critical preference that allows you to decide the final results in their adventure.

8. The reward: after overcoming the closing venture, the hero gets a reward or revelation that permits them to achieve their quest. This will be a latest records of themselves, a effective weapon, or the achievement in their preliminary aim.

nine. The avenue back: after acquiring their praise, the hero begins the journey decrease

decrease again to their everyday international. This adventure may be simply as hard due to the fact the preliminary journey, as they face new demanding situations and trials.

10. The pass again with the elixir: the move decrease back with the elixir is the instant whilst the hero comes lower lower back to their normal worldwide, wearing the reward or know-how received within the direction of their adventure. It additionally can be a second of battle decision and transformation for the hero and their surroundings.

The hero's adventure is a effective narrative model that resonates with readers as it reflects the challenges and trials all of us face in our own lives. By the use of the essential thing factors of the Hero's Journey narrative arc, you could create a fascinating and transferring story that touches your readers at their center.

Pay hobby to the settings to create colourful international

The settings and worlds wherein your characters navigate play a important role for your novel. Authentic and colourful settings can immerse your readers for your tale, letting them experience a wealthy and immersive journey. We will discover the significance of creating actual settings and offer you with guidelines to carry your fictional worlds to life.

1. Research and notion: to create real settings, research is crucial. Immerse your self within the life-style, statistics, shape, and landscapes of the location in which your novel takes place. Whether it's a actual or fictional area, draw notion from concrete statistics to lend credibility in your placing.

2. The 5 senses: undergo in mind to use the 5 senses to offer an cause of your settings. By depicting smells, sounds, tastes, textures, and shades, you could immerse your readers on your international in a sensory and immersive manner.

three. Balance between records and imagination: it is vital to provide data to create a vibrant putting, but keep away from overwhelming your readers with useless statistics. Leave room for his or her imagination if you need to create their non-public vision of the world you describe.

4. Consistency: make sure that the settings you describe are constant with the universe of your novel. Details need to align with the time period, social context, and way of lifestyles wherein your story unfolds.

five. Unique elements: create unique and various factors to your settings. Whether it's miles a geographical characteristic, a cultural way of lifestyles, or particular shape, those specific factors will deliver your international its personal character and originality.

6. The function of settings within the plot: settings can play an energetic feature for your novel's plot. They can be limitations to triumph over, belongings of concept, or reflections of the characters' emotions.

Integrate your settings meaningfully into your story to motive them to an critical element of your narrative.

7. Evolution of settings: surely as your characters evolve all through the tale, your settings can also trade. Settings can be suffering from the characters' actions or the improvement of the plot. Ensure you mirror those adjustments in your descriptions.

eight. Fantastic worlds: if your novel is prepared in a fantastical or imaginary international, make certain to create everyday policies and criminal guidelines governing this international. Describe creatures, cultures, and social systems in element to make this global credible and charming.

9. Emotional length of settings: settings can also have an emotional length. Use them to beautify the mood or emotion of a scene. For example, a dark and eerie setting should make stronger a experience of tension or worry, at the identical time as a vibrant and

heat placing can evoke a feeling of comfort or satisfaction.

10. Leave room for imagination: endure in mind to go away room on your readers' creativeness. Describe your settings sufficiently to reason them to tremendous, however do now not offer each element. Allow your readers to find out and bear in mind your global of their private manner.

By growing actual and colorful settings, you may add an additional size to your novel and invite your readers to certainly immerse themselves to your story. Well-constructed worlds can transport your readers into unforgettable adventures and captivate them till the final web web page.

Making your characters communicate with impactful communicate

Dialogue is an essential element of your novel. It breathes existence into your characters, revealing their personalities, feelings, and motivations. Impactful dialogues can captivate your readers, immerse them in the story, and encourage an attachment to the characters. Let's discover the art of crafting memorable and effective dialogues.

1. Authenticity of voices: each individual ought to have a one in every of a type voice that shows their person, upbringing, and social context. Listen to how people speak in actual lifestyles and encompass these nuances into your characters' dialogues to motive them to actual.

2. Subtext and the unsaid: dialogues do no longer continuously need to right now screen characters' feelings or intentions. Subtext, the unspoken factors a number of the strains, provides intensity to exchanges among characters.

3. Conciseness: impactful dialogues are regularly concise and direct. Avoid overly prolonged sentences or redundancies. Choose precise terms that correctly supply the emotions and intentions of the characters.

four. Importance of pauses and silences: pauses and silences in dialogues can be as effective as the phrases themselves. They can deliver hesitation, ache, or emotional tension. Use them appropriately to enhance the impact of your exchanges.

five. Rhythm and cadence: dialogues need to have a herbal rhythm that indicates the nuances of spoken language. Use versions in tone, pace, and cadence to make your dialogues sensible and attractive.

6. Emotional reactions: dialogues provide an opportunity to reveal the emotional reactions of your characters. Describe their facial expressions, gestures, and frame language to enhance the feelings conveyed through their phrases.

Chapter 4: Discovering Your Writing Fashion

The writing style is the signature of every author. It is what will make you particular and recognizable. Finding your writing fashion is vital to create a completely unique novel and depart a protracted-lasting effect on your readers. We will discover the importance of writing style and offer you with hints to boom a voice that is tremendously yours.

1. Authenticity: be yourself for your writing. Avoid seeking to imitate the varieties of particular authors or conforming to pre-mounted norms. Your authenticity is what is going to make your writing honest and endearing.

2. Clarity: a easy and fluid writing fashion is essential for effective communication in conjunction with your readers. Avoid overly complicated sentences or convoluted systems that would make your textual content difficult to recognize.

three. Word preference: the phrases you choose out have an impact on the temper and emotion of your novel. Opt for evocative and particular terms that seize the essence of what you need to express.

4. Musicality: the rhythm and musicality of your writing can create a fascinating atmosphere. Play with sounds, alliterations, and rhythms to provide your prose a melody that is appropriate to the ear.

5. Imagery and metaphors: use splendid imagery and powerful metaphors to carry your descriptions to existence and make your scenes more evocative. Strong snap shots stay anchored within the minds of readers.

6. Variety of syntax: variety the form of your sentences to create a dynamic rhythm for your writing. Short and impactful sentences can add dynamism to motion-packed moments, at the equal time as longer sentences and unique descriptions can supply a contemplative ecosystem.

7. Economy of phrases: reason to mention greater with much less. Avoid redundancies and needless words. Economy of phrases should make your prose extra impactful and inexperienced.

eight. Painter's metaphor: accept as true with your self as a painter with phrases. Use your writing style to create seen canvases that transport your readers into your worldwide.

9. Revision and experimentation: finding your writing style may be an evolving tool. Take the time to revise and test with unique strategies. This manner, you will find out what works brilliant for you.

10. Confidence to your voice: bear in mind on your creator's voice. Your style is precise, and that's what will make your novel specific. Do not doubt your functionality to captivate readers together with your special pen.

Finding your writing fashion takes time and workout, however it's miles an essential step in growing a unique that shows your innovative imaginative and prescient. Let your specific pen express itself freely and manual your readers within the direction of enchanting literary horizons.

How to put together your writing way

Writing a totally specific may be a daunting task, but with specific enterprise and a solid conflict plan, you could turn this innovative journey right right into a smoother and further efficient approach. We'll find out the importance of enterprise on your writing technique and provide you with techniques to create an effective artwork plan.

1. Set easy goals: in advance than starting your writing, installation smooth and viable dreams for your novel. Whether it is the amount of phrases you want to gain every day or the final touch date of your first draft, tangible dreams will assist you live on course eventually of the way.

2. Create a time desk: boom a time table in your writing technique. Break down the

venture into stages and set sensible closing dates for each degree, from planning to drafting, to revising. A time table will preserve you organized and song your improvement.

3. Find your writing everyday: turn out to be privy to the times of day whilst you're most modern-day and green, and create a writing everyday round those moments. Whether it's miles morning, afternoon, or nighttime, locate the time that fits you nice to write down down regularly. For instance, it is probably difficult to put in writing after a meal due to digestion, so it's far higher to time table different time slots for writing.

four. Eliminate distractions: pick out out distractions that can prevent your writing technique and take measures to dispose of them. Turn off phone notifications, find out a quiet area to jot down down, and absolutely attention to your artwork.

five. Fast draft technique: while writing your first draft, do not prevent to perfect every sentence. Use the short draft technique by using the use of specializing in advancing the tale with out worrying about facts. You'll have the possibility to refine your text all through the revision.

6. Keep song of mind: keep a pocket e-book or virtual document accessible to put in writing any thoughts that come to thoughts, despite the fact that they're no longer right now associated with your present day-day novel. These mind can also want to expose beneficial in the future or for different responsibilities.

7. Take everyday breaks: don't forget to take regular breaks throughout your writing manner. These moments of relaxation will recharge you, permitting you to go once more on your art work with a brisker and greater innovative mind.

8. Revise and edit little by little: at some point of revision and enhancing, technique your novel little by little. Start through way of checking the general shape, then circulate immediately to individual consistency, talk,

and in the long run, proofreading and fashion development.

nine. Seek outside comments: have others, consisting of pals, own family participants, or fellow writers, look at your novel to get outdoor feedback. Constructive remarks will allow you to come to be privy to strengths and weaknesses on your textual content and improve it.

10. Celebrate your achievements: each completed degree for your writing method deserves to be celebrated. Take the time to congratulate yourself on your improvement, whether it's far completing the planning, finishing the primary draft, or finalizing the manuscript. Celebrating your achievements will inspire you to hold moving in advance.

By organizing your writing way and developing a strong conflict plan, you deliver your self the terrific hazard of successfully finishing your novel project. Be regular, perseverant, and bendy in your technique, and your unique writing style will manual you in the path of the accomplishment of your literary work.

The first draft of your novel

The first draft of your novel is a vital step on your writing technique. It's the on the spot at the same time as you placed your mind on paper for the number one time and allow your creativeness run wild. Launching into writing with out fear is crucial to unharness your creativity and convey your tale to existence. We'll find out the significance of the number one draft and provide you with recommendations to dive in with out hesitation.

1. Unleash your creativity: within the first draft, do not censor yourself. Let your creativity go with the glide freely and write without traumatic approximately errors or perfection. Corrections and improvements will come later, as soon as you have got finished your first draft.

2. Write regularly: to make development on your first draft, commit to writing regularly, whether or not it's far every day, numerous times in line with week, or on a hard and rapid schedule. This difficulty will help you hold modern momentum and boom for your narrative.

3. Don't prevent to correct: during the number one draft, avoid stopping to correct every sentence or paragraph. The cause is to move speedy via your story, even though it approach leaving spelling mistakes or awkward sentences.

4. Trust your instincts: pay attention on your author's instinct. If an concept involves you whilst writing, discover it and permit your self be amazed with the beneficial useful resource of the commands your story takes. Be open to changes and unexpected twists.

5. Face your fears: writing a primary draft can evoke fears and doubts. Face them with the beneficial resource of reminding your self that this initial model is best an area to start, and

you could have the possibility to revise and enhance it later.

6. Accept imperfection: your first draft will now not be perfect, and that's simply ordinary. Accept imperfection as an inevitable element of the writing procedure. You'll have the opportunity to refine and polish your narrative during the revision and enhancing ranges.

7. Stay targeted on the tale: sooner or later of the first draft, deliver hobby to the essence of your tale. Let the narrative convey you and do not get distracted with the useful resource of manner of information. You'll have time to refine descriptions and characters later.

8. Celebrate every improvement: each step forward for your first draft is a fulfillment in itself. Celebrate each completed degree, whether or not it's miles finishing a financial catastrophe, meeting a key character, or exploring an critical scene. These celebrations will inspire you to preserve.

nine. Find assist: are looking for for manual from other writers, critique groups, or on-line forums. Sharing your improvement and disturbing situations with others who recognize the u.S.And downs of writing can be a valuable deliver of encouragement.

10. Trust the technique: the writing approach is particular for each author. Trust your very own technique and do now not look at yourself to others. Be affected individual and chronic because of the fact the first draft is the start of an thrilling adventure toward knowledge your novel.

Launching fearlessly into the primary draft is an essential step in bringing your story to existence. Enjoy this progressive freedom and encompass the journey that awaits you. The first draft is the foundation of your novel, and from there, you can gather, refine, and redesign your narrative proper into a excellent literary paintings.

Chapter 5: The Infamous Writer's Block Syndrome

Writing blocks and the feared smooth net web page are disturbing situations that every one writers face in some unspecified time within the destiny. However, there are powerful techniques to triumph over the ones barriers and rediscover your concept. We'll discover the importance of handling writing blocks and offer you with strategies to conquer the easy page.

1. writing habitual: installation a everyday writing routine. Sitting down on the identical time every day or week to install writing can scenario your thoughts to trade to modern mode at the ones instances.

2. Free writing: exercise unfastened writing to unleash your creativity. Choose a random assignment be counted or word and write with out interruption for a tough and fast duration. This can free up thoughts and feelings you could no longer find out otherwise.

3. Physical exercising: engage in normal bodily workout to beautify your energy and creativity. A brief walk or workout session can help alleviate strain and smooth your mind.

four. Meditation and mindfulness: exercising meditation or mindfulness to refocus and calm your thoughts. These strategies can help overcome tension associated with writing and assist you to attention at the winning 2d.

5. Change of environment: in case you sense caught, alternate your environment. Write in a café, a park, or maybe each different room in your home. A exchange of scenery can stimulate your creativity.

6. Inspirational reading: read works that encourage and encourage you. A superb study can purpose mind and make you keen to go lower lower back to writing.

7. Music and ambient sounds: use music or ambient sounds to create a writing-first-rate atmosphere. Certain tune or sounds let you

recognition and immerse your self to your writing international.

8. Non-judgmental writing: whilst going via the clean page, write with out judgment. Allow yourself to write down down some thing, despite the truth that it seems mundane or awkward. The secret is to start and allow the phrases go along with the flow.

nine. Set small goals: if the smooth internet page paralyzes you, set small writing goals. For example, inform your self you could write actually one internet page or perhaps a paragraph. Once you have got started out, it is regularly much less complicated to preserve.

10. Participate in writing worrying situations: be part of on line writing demanding situations or creator corporations. These traumatic situations provide prompts or constraints that let you smash loose from the clean internet internet web page.

Remember that writing blocks are an vital a part of the cutting-edge approach. Be kind to yourself and be open to exploring special techniques to conquer those boundaries. The key is to persevere and keep writing, even though it appears hard. Over time and with workout, you could increase personal techniques to triumph over the easy internet page and breathe existence into your boldest mind.

Revising your manuscript to enhance it

Revision is a critical step within the writing procedure. It's the instant at the same time as you step once more from your novel, have a look at its strengths and weaknesses, and make the essential improvements to make it shine. We'll explore the significance of clever revision and offer you with guidelines to effectively enhance your manuscript.

1. Gain mindset: while you start the revision technique, take a step another time from your novel. Let it rest for a few days or

possibly weeks to benefit a smooth and goal mind-set in your artwork.

2. Analyze the structure: check that your novel's form is coherent and logical. Ensure that sports glide easily and transitions among chapters are properly-completed.

3. Develop your characters: refine your characters with the useful resource of giving them more intensity and nuance. Ensure they have got clear and realistic motivations, and verify that they evolve constantly at some diploma in the tale.

4. Polish dialogues: evaluation your dialogues to guide them to sharp and proper. Eliminate repetitions and useless phrases, making sure that dialogues replicate absolutely everyone's person.

5. Refine language: be aware of the first-rate of language to your novel. Seek greater fashionable and evocative phraseology, put off clichés and overused expressions.

6. Control the pace: the pace of your novel is crucial for maintaining reader engagement. Alternate among motion scenes and quieter moments to create a dynamic rhythm.

7. Avoid inconsistencies: check for inconsistencies within the tale, characters, or settings. Pay hobby to information to create a coherent and credible narrative.

8. Seek outside remarks: have your manuscript observe with the resource of beta readers or publishing specialists to collect superb feedback. External opinions can help you discover strengths and weaknesses on your novel.

nine. Revise in multiple passes: do now not hesitate to revise your novel in a couple of passes, specializing in precise elements at some stage in every reread. For instance, have one skip devoted to dialogues and any other to the general form.

10. Know while to prevent: revision can be an endless undertaking if you do not recognize

on the same time as to prevent. Set cut-off dates for every revision degree, and recall that absolute perfection is hardly ever viable.

Revision is annoying artwork, however it's miles vital to provide your novel the essential polish in advance than sharing it with the area. Be affected man or woman, chronic, and open to modifications, as revision is an opportunity to make your particular writing style shine.

Soliciting and receiving reviews to enhance your novel

Critique is an inevitable part of the writing technique, and it could be each enriching and hard to virtually take shipping of. Knowing the manner to reap and offer optimistic comments is vital for reinforcing your novel and supporting fellow writers in their paintings. We will find out the significance of the art of critique and provide advice to make it a exquisite and powerful revel in.

1. Approach opinions with an open mind: at the same time as receiving feedback on your novel, hold an open mind and be prepared to just accept opinions terrific from your very very own. Remember that evaluations are there to help you apprehend weaknesses for your paintings and make it higher.

2. Don't take evaluations for my part: it's miles herbal to sense a few emotion in reaction to critiques, but attempt not to take them individually. Separate your identity as a writer from comments for your art work. Critiques purpose to beautify your novel, not devalue you.

3. Seek clarifications: if a few feedback are doubtful or go away you perplexed, do not hesitate to trying to find clarifications. Fully information reviews will let you practice them more effectively to beautify your novel.

4. Identify strengths and weaknesses: whilst receiving comments, choose out the strengths of your novel to capitalize on them. Similarly,

pinpoint weaknesses to target them sooner or later of the revision way.

5. Look for great truth: no longer all remarks is probably applicable or helpful. Look for exceptional criticism that aids in improving your writing, even though it could be hard to pay attention.

6. Avoid defensiveness: withstand the urge to shield your self or without delay reject reviews. Take time to assimilate and objectively hold in thoughts them earlier than reacting.

7. Provide positive feedback: whilst giving feedback to different writers, be high-quality and respectful. Focus on strengths as an entire lot as weaknesses and offer concrete suggestions to beautify their art work.

8. Identify areas of cognizance: in advance than offering comments, select out precise components to pay hobby on, which incorporates characters, narration, writing

style, and so forth. This will make your remarks more focused and useful.

9. Offer solutions, no longer clearly issues: instead of really citing problems, additionally suggest capability answers. This shows which you care approximately improving the opportunity writer's artwork.

10. Respect the writer's possibilities: every author has their own imaginative and prescient and writing fashion. Respect the writer's opportunities and avoid on the lookout for to pressure them to put in writing in step with your personal tastes.

The artwork of critique is a valuable talents for every author. Receiving constructive remarks permits you decorate your work, at the same time as providing optimistic remarks to specific writers strengthens the literary community. Well-managed critique contributes on your improvement as a author and that of fellow authors with whom you percent your passion.

Polishing your novel with a 2nd draft

The 2nd draft is a essential level. It lets in you to polish your novel and make it even more charming to your readers. It's the moment even as you revisit your story, thinking about the remarks acquired and refining every detail to excellent your narrative. We'll find out the importance of the second one draft and offer you with recommendations on sharpening your novel with care.

1. Consider feedback: if you acquired feedback from beta readers or exclusive writers at a few degree in the first revision, take it under interest on your 2nd draft. External comments can assist apprehend areas for improvement.

2. Check consistency: make certain your story is ordinary from beginning to surrender. Check information which includes man or woman names, places, and dates, ensuring they wholesome in the course of the unconventional.

three. Fine-song your characters: take gain of the second one draft to similarly refine your characters. Give them particular person tendencies, delve into their motivations, and make certain their movements and reactions are normal with their improvement.

4. Enhance the narration: art work on the narration of your novel to make descriptions greater vibrant and scenes extra evocative. Use effective imagery and evocative metaphors to immerse your readers on your international.

five. Revise the shape: take a look at the shape of your novel and make certain that chapters and scenes float effects. Identify additives that require adjustments or reorganization to bolster the tempo of your narrative.

6. Eliminate linguistic inconsistencies: search for grammatical errors, spelling errors, and linguistic inconsistencies. Clean and polished writing is vital for the credibility of your novel.

7. Make your dialogues impactful: refine dialogues to lead them to extra impactful and right. Eliminate repetitions and useless exchanges, making sure that dialogues mirror the tone and person of anyone.

eight. Work on the rhythm: be aware of the rhythm of your novel. Alternate movement-packed moments with quieter scenes to maintain the reader's hobby in some unspecified time within the destiny of the narrative.

9. Seek feedback: have your second draft reviewed with the aid of the usage of beta readers or publishing experts to accumulate more insights in advance than finalizing your manuscript.

Chapter 6: Beta Readers To Acquire Treasured Remarks

Beta Readers play a critical function within the writing method through providing precious comments in your novel. These are voluntary readers who take a look at your manuscript earlier than its e-book and offer their impressions, opinions, and tips. We will find out the significance of beta readers and provide you with recommendations to accumulate valuable feedback in your work.

1. Choose your beta readers carefully: pick beta readers who are inquisitive about your literary style and are willing to provide positive and honest remarks. Opt for lots of readers to gain severa views.

2. Define your expectations: in advance than handing your manuscript to beta readers, certainly outline your expectations. Specify the type of remarks you are seeking out, together with comments at the plot, characters, writing fashion, and so on.

three. Be open to criticism: acquire comments out of your beta readers with an open mind. Remember that their goal is to help you enhance your novel, and once in a while this entails optimistic grievance.

four. Collect written remarks: ask your beta readers to offer written comments because it permits you to make the effort to analyze it in element and use it on your revision.

five. Organize discussions: further to written remarks, prepare person or corporation discussions together together with your beta readers. This will allow you to delve into unique elements of your novel and better recognize their reactions.

6. Identify trends: whilst reading comments from your beta readers, search for tendencies and habitual styles. This will help you discover the strengths of your novel, further to regions that need development.

7. Ask unique questions: have your beta readers solution specific questions about high

quality factors of your novel. This can assist them reputation their comments and provide you with extra targeted records.

eight. Accept variety of critiques: each beta reader may have a selected opinion in your novel. Accept the type of reactions and do not try to please all people. Take under consideration the remarks that resonates along with your authorial vision.

nine. Express gratitude: show your gratitude in your beta readers for the time and effort they committed to analyzing your manuscript and providing remarks. This will inspire their destiny participation.

10. Make knowledgeable choices: whilst revising your novel thinking about the remarks from beta readers, make knowledgeable selections. Assimilate the feedback, but keep in mind that you are the author, and the very last selection is yours.

Beta readers are valuable allies on your quest to improve your novel. By cautiously being attentive to their comments and the use of it to guide your revision, you can first-rate your artwork and make it greater appealing on your future readers.

Crafting strong moments with captivating scenes

Key moments are the pivotal scenes of your novel, folks who captivate your readers, stir their emotions, and maintain them on the edge in their seats until the forestall. Creating fascinating scenes is essential to maintain your readers' hobby and immerse them completely on your story. We'll discover the importance of key moments and provide you with recommendations to craft unforgettable scenes.

1. Identify key moments: earlier than you start writing, become aware about the vital detail moments of your story. These are the essential sports that stress the plot in advance and characteristic an effect at the characters.

2. Increase tension: key moments are regularly laden with emotional anxiety. Increase anxiety with the aid of putting your characters in hard conditions, developing conflicts, and dilemmas that compel them to behave.

three. Be visible and sensory: make your scenes captivating with the aid of way of being visible and sensory for your descriptions. Use facts that stimulate your readers' senses and plunge them into the coronary coronary heart of the motion.

four. Play with feelings: key moments need to evoke feelings in your readers. Play with their feelings with the aid of manner of the use of growing moving, surprising, or suspenseful scenes.

5. Use talk efficiently: communicate is a effective device to make your scenes captivating. Use it to show vital statistics, display relationships among characters, and decorate the plot.

6. Create plot twists: marvel your readers via incorporating plot twists into your key moments. These unexpected turns can create emotional shocks and maintain the reader's attention.

7. Build a dynamic rhythm: key moments need to have a dynamic rhythm to hold the reader's interest. Alternate amongst calm moments and motion scenes to create stability in your narrative.

8. Ensure selection: key moments have to deliver resolution to conflicts and dilemmas supplied. Ensure that every scene has an effect on the general story and contributes to the characters' development.

9. Leave an emotional impact: key moments are folks who linger inside the reader's mind prolonged after completing the novel. Aim to go away a strong emotional impact by means of growing memorable scenes.

10. Reread and refine: as soon as you have written your key moments, reread and refine

them. Ensure they'll be nicely included into everything of your narrative and upload price for your novel.

Key moments are vital pillars of your novel. They are the moments even as your tale comes to existence, and your readers are really immersed on your universe. By growing charming scenes, you make certain an unforgettable reading experience in your target audience.

An emotional contact to stir your readers

The emotional contact is the very essence of a fascinating novel. It's what resonates alongside aspect your readers, touches them on the center, and leaves them with immoderate feelings lengthy after they've closed your e-book. We'll discover the importance of the emotional touch and offer you with recommendations to stir your readers via your writing.

1. Create endearing characters: nicely-superior and endearing characters are key to

evoking feelings for your readers. Make your characters human, with strengths, weaknesses, hopes, and fears.

2. Show vulnerability: permit your characters to reveal their vulnerability. Readers regularly connect more with characters going thru complex emotions and personal disturbing situations.

three. Use emotional language: select phrases and terms that evoke emotions. Employ evocative descriptions, powerful metaphors, and expressions that contact your readers' hearts.

four. Explore some of feelings: do now not restrict yourself to a single emotion. Explore the entire spectrum of human emotions, from delight to unhappiness, worry to like, anger to wish. This will make your tale richer and extra nuanced.

5. Create immoderate moments: craft excessive moments for your novel—folks who make your readers' hearts beat faster, depart

them breathless, or engulf them in sturdy emotions.

6. Play with readers' feelings: play in conjunction with your readers' feelings with the aid of introducing emotional twists, surprising revelations, and coronary heart-wrenching dilemmas to your characters.

7. Show empathy: located yourself for your readers' footwear and recollect how your scenes and characters could likely for my part contact them. Empathy will help you create deeper emotional connections.

eight. Show, do not inform: show off your characters' feelings via their actions, gestures, and expressions in place of explaining them immediately to the reader. This makes emotions extra authentic and tangible.

nine. Let your emotion be right: bring your proper feelings in your writing. If you're moved at the same time as writing a scene, there may be a wonderful danger your readers might be moved at the same time as analyzing it.

10. Leave an emotional impact: cause to go away a long-lasting emotional impact in your readers. If your story deeply resonates with them, they'll recall your novel lengthy after completing it.

The emotional touch is what transforms an everyday novel into an superb experience for readers. Stirring readers with real emotions is the final purpose of each creator. By following the ones recommendations, you could create effective emotional connections that make your novel a memorable and sizeable enjoy for your readers.

Chapter 7: Handling Descriptions And Information

Balancing the information you offer to your readers is essential to maintain their interest and preserve them immersed to your tale. Dosing descriptions and statistics is a vital talent for developing fascinating narration with out dulls your readers. We will find out the significance of information balance and offer you with recommendations on exactly dosing descriptions and info for your novel.

1. Consider the fluidity of the narrative: whilst along side descriptions and info, make sure they absolutely integrate into the tale and do now not disrupt the float. Avoid data that feels artificially positioned.

2. Choose sizeable facts: select data which is probably large to the plot, characters, or the overall surroundings of your novel. Meaningful records make a contribution to the richness of the tale, at the identical time as useless information can weigh it down.

3. Use descriptions to create surroundings: descriptions are a powerful device for developing the atmosphere and environment of your tale. Appeal to the 5 senses to immerse your readers in the settings and emotions.

four. Avoid block statistics: steer clean of prolonged block descriptions which can come across as a listing of information. Integrate data organically, dispersing them thru movement and speak.

5. Respect the narrative pace: adjust the density of statistics based totally on the narrative pace. Fast-paced movement moments also can require fewer information, while calm moments can gain from extra in-depth descriptions.

6. Trust the reader's imagination: provide sufficient cues for the reader to visualize scenes and characters, however also depart room for the reader's imagination to engage with the tale.

7. Reveal info regularly: to keep reader interest, regularly display info due to the fact the plot unfolds. This maintains an element of mystery and sparks hobby.

8. Balance talk and descriptions: exchange among speak and outlines to energise your novel. Dialogues strength the plot beforehand and screen character emotions, at the equal time as descriptions improve the narrative universe.

9. Targeted revisions: within the route of the revision of your novel, pay unique interest to passages containing descriptions and information. Ensure they may be relevant and make a contribution to the overall story.

10. Be concise and evocative: cause for conciseness in your descriptions at the equal time as being evocative. Use effective phrases that create vibrant pictures inside the reader's mind.

Balancing descriptions and details is a matter of subtle dosage to captivate your readers all through your novel. A well-balanced dosage will permit your story to spread harmoniously, presenting readers an immersive and brilliant enjoy.

How to conquer barriers

The writing of a completely unique can be a profitable journey, but it's also common to come upon barriers that can discourage even the most passionate authors. We'll discover common obstacles writers face and provide strategies to triumph over them efficaciously.

1. Writer's block: author's block is a commonplace obstacle in which concept seems to dry up, and words refuse to return returned. To triumph over it, attempt stepping a ways from your assignment in brief, take a destroy, and engage in revolutionary activities to stimulate your creativeness.

2. Fear of failure: fear of failure can paralyze a author, stopping them from continuing their undertaking or sharing it with the world. To

conquer it, don't forget that failure is a part of the gaining knowledge of manner, and every obstacle is an opportunity to increase as a author.

three. Excessive perfectionism: aiming for perfection is commendable, but immoderate perfectionism can save you you from finishing your novel. Learn to allow bypass and be given that the number one draft won't be ideal; it can constantly be stepped forward for the duration of revisions.

4. Lack of time: locating time to write can be hard, specially with a hectic time table. Organize your schedule to encompass regular writing sessions, despite the fact that they'll be quick.

5. Self-doubt: it's miles normal to doubt your writing capabilities, however do now not permit the ones doubts keep you again. Remember that writing is an art work that improves with exercise, and every word you write brings you inside the direction of your cause.

6. Negative feedback: terrible remarks can be difficult to cope with, but do now not take it as a thinking of your honestly absolutely well worth as a writer. Use it as possibilities for studying and boom to beautify your work.

7. Lack of motivation: motivation can waver, but retaining a ordinary writing location is essential for progressing on your project. Find belongings of thought, including analyzing one of a kind authors, to reignite your motivation.

8. Comparisons with unique writers: comparing yourself to other writers can be discouraging, particularly if you revel in inferior. Remember that every writer has their private journey and precise fashion, and you've your voice to offer to the place.

nine. Distractions: distractions like social media, tv, or own family chores can divert your interest from writing. Create a conducive writing surroundings via eliminating distractions and use time manipulate machine to live centered.

10. Lack of self-self assurance: having self-self warranty is essential for advancing as a author. Work in your arrogance and apprehend which you have the right to tell your tale and percentage your ideas with the arena.

Every impediment you stumble upon as a writer can be an opportunity to expand and decorate. By adopting a first rate thoughts-set closer to disturbing situations and developing strategies to overcome them, you could keep your writing journey with resilience and backbone.

Chapter 8: The Ebook Of Your Novel

The e book of your novel is an exciting and important step for your writing adventure. There are severa alternatives for publishing your novel, every with its private advantages and disturbing conditions. We will explore the simplest-of-a-kind paths of publishing available to you to percent your artwork with the vicinity.

1. Traditional publishing: conventional publishing is the conventional course, in which you placed up your manuscript to publishing houses. If your novel is ordinary, the publishing residence takes care of the complete publishing approach, from cowl format to ebook distribution in shops. Traditional publishing gives professional validation and may offer more visibility, however the desire technique may be extended and competitive.

2. Vanity publishing: vanity publishing involves finding out to buy the ebook of your novel. You finance the layout, layout, and

printing of the e-book yourself. This preference is commonly now not encouraged except there may be a particular motive that aligns at the side of your alternatives. Make sure to pick out a very good conceitedness publishing house this is apparent in its services.

3. Self-publishing: self-publishing has grow to be increasingly more famous with the rise of on-line self-publishing structures together with amazon's kindle direct publishing (kdp). With self-publishing, you have got got got complete control over the publishing gadget, from cover layout to digital and print distribution. It is a brief and available choice, but it also calls for more art work in terms of advertising and marketing and marketing to acquire your audience.

four. Hybrid publishing: hybrid publishing houses provide a mixture of traditional and self-publishing. They may provide expert modifying services for a charge but moreover pick a few manuscripts for conventional publishing. Conduct thorough research and thoroughly have a look at the phrases of the agreement earlier than choosing this feature.

5. Digital publishing (e-book): publishing your novel as an ebook is a short and fee-powerful preference, whether or now not through self-publishing or a digital publishing residence. E-books are easy to distribute and can achieve a huge on-line target audience. Ensure that your novel is nicely formatted for numerous e-reading structures.

6. Collaborative publishing: collaborative publishing houses are agencies that provide expert improving services for a price but do no longer require an in advance fee. They then percentage the sales from e-book earnings. Be careful and examine the agreement terms cautiously earlier than selecting this feature, as a few collaborative publishing homes may additionally lack integrity.

7. Print on call for: with print on demand, books are found out as wanted, meaning

there can be no bodily stock. This enables lessen printing prices and avoids unsold stock.

Before deciding on the publishing direction that fits you, make an effort to investigate and apprehend the alternatives available. Each route has its specialists and cons, and what topics most is finding the one that aligns terrific in conjunction with your desires as a author. Be vigilant about the content cloth material of any contracts you could enter into.

Chapter 9: Focus On Self-Publishing To Launch

Self-publishing is an more and more famous desire for authors who need to preserve complete manipulate over their paintings and speedy get admission to the marketplace. However, launching as an independent creator calls for correct enough training and business company. We will study the crucial steps to attain yourself-publishing journey as an impartial writer.

1. Refine your manuscript: earlier than delving into self-publishing, make certain that your manuscript is ready. Review, revise, and characteristic your textual content proofread through beta readers to ensure the first-rate of your novel.

2. Design an attractive cover: the cover is a essential element to attract readers. If you lack photograph format abilities, remember hiring a professional to create an attractive and expert cowl.

3. Format your e-book for e-book and print: make sure that your novel is effectively formatted for both e-book and print versions. Self-publishing systems, collectively with Kindle Direct Publishing (KDP), offer courses and templates to help you on this mission.

four. Choose distribution structures: pick out out distribution structures to your ebook and posted ebook. Amazon's KDP is one of the maximum popular alternatives, but there are also different structures which embody Kobo Writing Life, Apple Books, and IngramSpark for print on name for.

5. Set a competitive sale price: decide the promoting fee of your e-book based totally absolutely honestly in your literary fashion, the length of your novel, and the expenses set by using way of the usage of various comparable authors. Strike the right stability among attracting readers and incomes an affordable profits.

6.Implement A selling technique: vending is essential to make your ebook stated. Create an writer website or weblog, use social media, take part in literary activities, solicit reviews, and be lively within the on line literary community. You can also undergo in thoughts advertising.

7. Craft compelling e-book description and income internet page: the define of your e-book and your income net web page are important to persuade readers to shop for. Write a catchy description that introduces the plot and captures the reader's hobby.

eight. Leverage to be had resources: take advantage of sources available to impartial authors, which embody on-line guide agencies, self-publishing blogs, education, and webinars. Learn from other authors and share your critiques with the network.

nine. Be affected man or woman and continual: self-publishing also can take effort and time earlier than your ebook unearths its audience. Be affected person and persistent, and preserve to sell your ebook even after its preliminary release.

10. Monitor typical performance and adapt: maintain a watch on your e-book's overall performance and reader comments. If important, make enhancements to your novel or promoting approach based totally totally mostly on the comments acquired.

Self-publishing offers impartial authors the liberty and opportunity to percentage their memories with a tremendous target audience. By following the ones steps, you may be on the path to achievement in yourself-publishing journey and great your dream of becoming a finished impartial writer.

Designing an attractive cowl to growth income

The cowl of your e book is the number one impact readers will have of your novel. An attractive cowl can pique the hobby of readers, entice them to discover your story, and in the long run, prompt them to make a purchase. We will find out the vital elements for designing a cowl that sells and grabs the attention of your target audience.

1. Understand your target audience: Before designing your cowl, it is vital to recognize your target marketplace. Identify the demographic characteristics of your functionality readers, their pursuits, and the literary genres they revel in. This will assist you create a cover that meets their expectations.

2. Capture the essence of the radical: The cover want to reflect the essence of your novel. It need to supply readers an concept of the literary genre, temper, and plot of your story. Choose seen elements that as it should be represent the content of your ebook.

3. Opt for professional layout: If you lack picture layout abilities, hold in thoughts hiring a professional to create your cowl. Professional format offers an have an effect on of great and credibility on your ebook, that would encourage readers to take an hobby.

4. Care for the perceive and writer: The become aware of and creator's call need to be clean and with out issues readable on the quilt. Choose fonts suitable for the literary fashion and make certain they stand out properly towards the ancient past photograph.

five. Use placing images: The images you choose out on your cover want to be placing and appealing. Avoid low-selection pics and make sure they are consistent with the content of your e-book.

6. Work on colour concord: Colors play a sizeable function in the seen enchantment of your cowl. Opt for harmonious hues that complement every unique well. Avoid garish colors that is probably unpleasant for readers.

7. Create a balanced composition: The composition of your cowl want to be balanced and well-primarily based. Ensure that visible factors, together with pics, titles, and subtitles, are positioned coherently and aesthetically.

eight. Avoid information overload: Do now not muddle your cover with too much facts. A clean and easy layout is often extra powerful in grabbing the attention of readers.

nine. Test reader reactions: Before finalizing your cowl, are looking for for the evaluations of beta readers or buddies. Their reactions can provide insights into the effectiveness of your format.

10. Adapt the quilt to codecs: Ensure that your cowl is suitable for all codecs wherein your ebook might be posted, whether or now not or not it is for e-books, print versions, or social media.

The cover of your ebook is a display off that encourages readers to take an interest for your novel. By designing an attractive cowl, you increase the opportunities of charming your target market and giving your e-book progressed visibility. Remember that the number one have an effect on counts, and your cover is step one towards the achievement of your novel.

Chapter 10: Advertising And Marketing

Promotion is a important step to make your e book mentioned and achieve your audience. Smart advertising will assist you create advanced visibility for your novel and trap the eye of functionality readers. We'll discover effective and clever vending techniques to make your e book shine.

1. Establish an internet presence: assemble a web presence by using way of way of growing an writer net website on-line or blog wherein you could display off your e-book, percentage excerpts, and have interaction together along with your readers. Use social media to gain a miles broader audience.

2. Leverage social media: social media is a powerful tool to sell your ebook. Share relevant content material, interact along facet your target market, and create targeted advertising and marketing campaigns to generate interest amongst readers.

3. Reach out to bloggers and reviewers: are searching out reviews from literary bloggers

and online ebook reviewers. Positive reviews can capture the eye of functionality readers and decorate the credibility of your ebook.

four. Host contests: arrange contests on social media to encourage reader engagement and create buzz spherical your ebook. Offer signed copies, goodies, or top notch reminiscences as prizes.

five. Collaborate with other authors: accomplice with authors for your literary fashion to installation joint activities, e-book signings, or bypass-promotional interviews. This mutual collaboration will assist you to acquire new readers.

6. Capitalize on advertising and advertising and marketing opportunities: take gain of advertising and advertising opportunities which include promotions on e-book structures, focused social media advertising, and advertisements in literary publications.

7. Participate in ebook fairs and literary sports: attend e-book gala's, exchange

indicates, and literary sports to fulfill readers in person, network with one of a kind company specialists, and promote your ebook.

eight. Create fantastic content fabric: produce first-rate content on subjects associated with your e-book and literary universe. This can encompass weblog articles, films, podcasts, or infographics. Interesting content material cloth fabric can attraction to readers inquisitive about your art work.

9. Engage in online literary corporations: be part of boards, facebook businesses, and on-line literary companies in which you can share your ardour for writing and have interaction with readers who proportion similar pursuits.

10. Communicate regularly on the side of your readers: hold ordinary conversation at the facet of your readers with the aid of sending newsletters, responding to their feedback on social media, and giving them a in the returned of-the-scenes glimpse into your writing technique.

Smart advertising and marketing is a aggregate of on-line and offline efforts to create most visibility for your e-book. By using those smart vending techniques, you may generate buzz round your novel, capture the attention of your target marketplace, and construct a community of loyal readers.

Useful software program and applications for writing

In the technique of writing a completely unique, writing system can be of top notch help in organizing, stimulating creativity, and enhancing productiveness. We'll discover a number of the maximum beneficial software software and programs for authors, making the writing technique more possible and permitting you to cognizance at the essence of your tale.

1. Word processing software application: phrase processing software program software software like Microsoft Word, Google Docs, or Scrivener is vital for drafting your novel. It permits you to write, revise, and layout your

textual content professionally. In our case, we're advocates of LibreOffice Writer.

2. Note-taking apps: have a look at-taking apps which encompass Evernote or OneNote are excellent for speedy taking images your thoughts, inspirations, and studies. You can use them for your pc, pill, or cellular telephone to maintain all your notes at your fingertips. Linux customers can also additionally select out the Basket Notes software.

three. Planning and commercial enterprise agency tools: making plans and enterprise system like Trello or Asana help you form your novel through developing assignment lists, forums, and calendars. They offer a top degree view of your assignment and allow you to track your improvement.

4. Time control apps: time control apps like Toggl or Pomodone assist you effectively control your writing time. They assist you to song the time spent on every challenge and

consciousness on committed writing durations.

5. Editing and revision equipment: editing and revision equipment collectively with Grammarly or ProWritingAid assist encounter and correct spelling, grammar, and style errors for your text. They may be beneficial in improving the extremely good of your writing. If you use LibreOffice Writer, you could beautify its correction and revision abilties with Grammalecte.

6. Distraction blocking apps: distraction-blocking apps like Freedom or Cold Turkey help you live targeted through the usage of in brief blocking get proper of entry to to distracting web internet sites and packages during your writing instructions.

7. Mind mapping: mind mapping equipment like XMind or MindMeister assist you arrange your ideas visually by means of the use of growing thoughts maps or diagrams that can encourage the improvement of your novel. FreeMind and FreePlane also are useful tool.

eight. Speech-to-text software program program software program: speech-to-text software application like Dragon NaturallySpeaking may be useful in case you choose out dictating your textual content in place of typing. It permits you to dictate your tale and notice it transcribed automatically.

nine. Project control apps: undertaking control apps like ClickUp or Notion are perfect if you artwork in a set or want to control more than one writing obligations simultaneously.

10. Cover format system: in case you pick out out self-publishing, cowl design system together with Canva or Adobe Spark permit you to layout an appealing cover for your ebook.

Choose the gadget that nice healthful your dreams and writing style. Writing tools may be valuable allies in optimizing your writing gadget, handling a while successfully, and improving the pleasant of your novel.

How to govern your writing time

Writing a unique requires time, perseverance, and effective time manipulate. Balancing your passion for writing with every day obligations may be a task, however with clever planning and organizational strategies, you may find the stableness amongst your private existence and your lifestyles as a author. We will discover techniques for efficaciously coping with your writing time and bringing your literary passion to life while assembly the wishes of truth.

1. Establish a everyday writing time desk: Set regular writing slots to your time table. Whether it is early in the morning, at some stage in lunch breaks, or in the night, developing a routine will help you've got interplay usually for your writing paintings.

2. Set practical writing goals: Set practicable and realistic writing desires. This may be a every day or weekly phrase depend or a specific every day writing length. Adhering in

your dreams will help you're making everyday development for your novel.

three. Identify intervals of productivity: Observe the instances of day whilst you are maximum green and innovative. Take advantage of these durations to dedicate yourself to writing your novel. If feasible, modify your time table to optimize the ones moments.

4. Eliminate distractions: Identify assets of distraction that could disrupt your writing time and take measures to take away them. Distance your self from social media, television, and different distractions that could prevent your interest.

five. Prioritize your passion for writing: Prioritize your passion for writing through using allocating time to write down down, notwithstanding the truth that it means making sacrifices in exclusive regions of your lifestyles. Make writing an important part of your each day normal.

6. Plan extended writing periods: Reserve longer writing intervals ultimately of your days off or free time periods. These prolonged moments will will permit you to enter a rustic of go together with the float and make big development to your novel.

7. Use breaks to contemplate your novel: Make use of lunch breaks or waiting times to ponder your novel and jot down mind. These brief moments of mirrored picture may be treasured for developing your story.

eight. Communicate collectively along with your assist network: Communicate along with your manual community about the importance of your ardour for writing and your need for time to write down. Involve them to your undertaking and are searching for their assist to assist protect your writing moments.

nine. Be bendy: Be bendy collectively with your writing time table. Life can be unpredictable, and it is vital to simply accept that changes may be important once in a while.

10. Find belief for your fact: Use research out of your each day lifestyles as a deliver of inspiration in your novel. The feelings, social interactions, and traumatic conditions you come across can beautify your writing.

By intelligently managing your writing time and finding a balance among your passion for writing and the wishes of truth, you may deliver your novel to life on the same time as flourishing in your personal and expert life.

Chapter 11: How To Enhance Your Competencies Over The Years

Writing is a perpetual studying technique, and an aspiring author evolves into an performed writer over time. We will discover the significance of non-stop studying, emphasizing the enhancement of your abilities, openness to new thoughts, and perseverance inside the face of traumatic situations.

1. Invest in getting to know: live open to gaining information of recent writing strategies, studying books on the art work of writing, and participating in writing workshops or online courses. Continuous analyzing will assist you refine your fashion and growth your literary horizons.

2. Read drastically: analyzing is an essential approach to attract thought and observe from one-of-a-type authors. Regularly look at books in brilliant genres to discover new voices, numerous writing patterns, and unique narrative approaches.

3. Embrace optimistic grievance: be open to superb feedback out of your readers, beta readers, or one-of-a-type authors. Honest comments will help you apprehend the strengths and weaknesses of your writing and beautify as a result.

four. Experiment with new genres and styles: don't be afraid to test with new genres and writing patterns. Stepping from your consolation sector permit you to boom your creativity and find out new aspects of your writing information.

five. Maintain a writing mag: keep a writing magazine to file your thoughts, thoughts, and writing reviews. This will assist you to tune your evolution as a creator and maintain a record of your literary adventure.

6. Set writing desires: installation precise and measurable writing desires to inspire yourself to development. Set realistic deadlines to finish chapters, duties, or acquire a fantastic word depend in step with day.

7. Reassess your previous artwork: every now and then, assume yet again your previous works to assess your improvement as a author. You is probably surprised with the resource of the evolution of your fashion and voice over the years.

8. Collaborate with distinctive writers: collaborate with one-of-a-kind writers for joint initiatives or organization writing intervals. Interactions with fellow authors can be a supply of perception, concept alternate, and mutual aid.

9. Embrace failure and persevere: be prepared to face failure and demanding situations to your writer's journey. Perseverance and the willingness to keep writing no matter barriers are important for growth and achievement.

10. Celebrate your successes: don't forget to have amusing your successes, massive or small. Every milestone carried out in your writing journey deserves birthday celebration as it motivates you to hold developing.

Considering yourself a perpetual learner is a treasured thoughts-set for a creator. Continuous learning allows for development and the advent of an increasing number of enriching and charming works.

Taking into interest readers' evaluations to become more potent

When you positioned up your novel, you open the door to comments from readers. Whether top notch or high quality, the ones feedback can be a precious deliver of information to enhance your writing and beautify your connection with your audience. We will explore the significance of reader feedback and a manner to use it to refine your craft as a writer.

1. Embrace complaint with an open thoughts: gather grievance with an open thoughts and without taking the comments individually. Remember that reader remarks is an opportunity for growth and improvement, not a private assessment of your in reality well worth as a writer.

2. Identify trends: even as you get preserve of numerous comparable opinions, pick out developments and ordinary troubles. This will assist you aim areas of your writing that require particular hobby.

three. Consider the opinion of your audience: be aware about the opinion of your target audience. Reader remarks out of your demographic can help you better recognize their expectations and selections.

4. Use nice complaint to beautify your writing: use high quality complaint to pick out weaknesses in your novel and art work on enhancing them. This can also embody revising tremendous passages, deepening character improvement, or refining your writing fashion.

5. Celebrate great remarks: recognize high quality comments and have fun your novel's successes. Praise will encourage you and offer the motivation to keep writing with ardour.

6. Don't be discouraged by means of the usage of terrible grievance: receiving bad grievance is inevitable, and it does now not mean your paintings lacks price. Don't be discouraged through such reviews; instead, use them as an opportunity to develop and enhance.

7. Request particular comments: in case you want remarks on precise elements of your novel, ask your readers or beta-readers for unique enter. This will will let you purpose particular areas you need to improve.

8. Strike a balance among mirrored picture and movement: even as receiving feedback, take time to reflect and step again in advance than selecting moves to take. Strike a balance among reflected picture and movement to make extensive upgrades to your novel.

9. Value the reviews of loyal readers: remarks from reliable readers is specially valuable as they're familiar in conjunction with your art work and may provide insightful perspectives to your evolution as a creator.

10. Believe in yourself and your voice: hold self notion in your self and your writer's voice, despite the fact that faced with grievance. It's your ardour, originality, and authenticity that make you a unique writer.

By using reader remarks as a manual to refine your writing, you can create novels that resonate greater deeply together together along with your audience and depart a long lasting have an effect on.

It's first-rate the start

The studying of this ebook is virtually the start of your journey as a author. It is as plenty as you to put in writing the continuation of your very very very own story.

We have simply explored the numerous elements of writing a singular, from the preliminary sparks of idea to publishing on Amazon thru KDP. We have addressed the annoying situations and opportunities that each author faces and shared realistic recommendation for overcoming boundaries.

You have delved into writing techniques, storytelling tips, and clever vending strategies to make your e-book shine.

Throughout this guide, you have determined that writing is a deep passion that connects you to your self and others. Your writing fashion and creativity make you an actual and valuable writer in your goal market. You have determined to be open to positive grievance, to encompass annoying conditions as possibilities to grow, and to have an remarkable time your successes.

Your adventure as a creator continues because of the truth there may be no final excursion spot in the art of writing. Every story you inform, each project you adopt, is an invitation to discover new frontiers, assignment your limits, and precise your passion.

Remember that each first-rate writer started somewhere, with a primary phrase, a primary paragraph, a primary financial disaster. The key is to hold writing, mastering, and growing.

Find concept in your normal existence, inside the people you meet, in the books you study, and in the dreams that inhabit your coronary heart.

No rely in which you're, never forget about that you have a very particular and important voice to proportion with the area. Write with ardour, write with love, and write with self perception. Keep writing, evolving, and telling stories that captivate and encourage your readers.

Chapter 12: Story Vs. Plot

Now which you're mentally organized to jot down down a e-book, you understand what genre you discover with and the writer you want to be. It's time to take a seat down (or stand if it absolutely is your problem) and writes a e-book. If you have got determined to define your plot, you recognize the course the tale is going to take. And if you want to permit your imagination run wild, you understand more or much less what the eBook you need to jot down down down is set.

But earlier than you start, you need to realize some fundamentals. Like the reality that a tremendous tale is a aggregate of a properly-drawn plot with a man or woman's inner tale. And that all books start with a strong hook and an inciting incident (Chapter 6). To recognize a way to craft those, you have to recognize the difference maximum of the story and the plot.

This is a complex concept, and if this turn out to be an educational e-book, I could probably let you know a few issue like this: "tale is the chronological collection of sports and plot is the causal and logical shape which connects the activities." But this definition is not enough that will help you write books that impact readers.

Literary agent Lisa Cron and writer Jessica Brody each agree that considered considered one of the maximum important mistakes novice writers make is writing books without a tale. This is due to the fact they confuse the tale with the plot. That's good enough. We've all been in that feature. Jessica Brody herself wrote her ebook Save the Cat! Writes a Novel after many publishers rejected her, saying she wrote properly however lacked story. And Lisa Cron wrote Story Genius to provide an explanation for the which means of tale. These books wouldn't gain fulfillment among writers if we didn't make this mistake all the time.

The trouble with this mixture-up is that many writers may also additionally have a incredible idea, however then they set vehicles exploding left and proper or make the heroine make mistake after mistake in her search for the prince with out ever telling us how all of this influences the characters internally. They don't know that story is a first rate deal more than the prose, the voice, the shape, or the plot. Or even that it isn't sufficient to have a logical form or a nicely-described series.

In the phrases of Lisa Cron, story is straight away intertwined with the precept character, how they make feel of what's happening and make alternatives that pressure the motion. Story is about how the plot influences the protagonist and the manner he or she evolves as a give up end result.

To located it simply, the plot is the collection of activities that take vicinity inside the tale. The out of doors trouble. And if you have already got an concept to your manuscript, you most likely apprehend what the plot of the ebook you need to write down down down is. You apprehend, that summary line or the answer you supply even as human beings ask you, what is your ebook about?

If I had to supply an cause of the plot of Sombras (Shadows), I may additionally say: it is approximately a scholar of folklore and mythology who is recruited by means of the use of the use of an employer that hunts supernatural creatures. This is the out of doors problem. And for lovers of the style, it would even keep their interest. But if I had been to put in writing the ebook focusing best on the gathering of activities:

Lilly loses her mother and father;

Lilly actions to each other u . S .;

Lilly is recruited through way of an business enterprise of supernatural hunters;

Lilly now fights supernatural beings...

...no character could get past the primary financial ruin.

None of these factors make the reader care about my individual. There are many books about characters who lose own family people, and there are unique books approximately characters who flow into to specific worldwide locations. Not all books talk approximately corporations looking supernatural beings, but none of this is going to have an effect in case you do not provide an reason for to the reader why they want to care. So some distance, in my scheme of factors, Lilly is a fictional idea. Why will all people select my ebook amongst such a lot of others?

For that to manifest, you need to make the person revel in actual, and also you want to make the reader care. As João Mancelos stated: it's now not about the motion. It's about the human beings. If your neighbor's pal's pal receives run over, you will probable say, "Oh, that's horrible precise fortune!" But if the equal occurs to at least one in each of your parents or siblings, you may possibly panic.

And the most crucial lesson I can teach you as a writer is that the plot wants to expect your man or woman. If you do not consciousness on making us care approximately your man or woman with the resource of the use of showing how the plot affects her, you could rip her whole family's heads off, make all her boyfriends abandon her, and damage her complete united states, and your reader will even though now not care. This is due to the fact the story specializes in the internal conflict. It's about the lesson the protagonist will should have a look at in coping with the outside plot trouble.

You should provide the reader someone to root for if you want to make your man or woman memorable and create the empathy on the way to make the reader want for the character to prevail. When you consider the outdoor sports activities which can be going to seem around your character, undergo in mind the manner it impacts them internally. If such an event has no impact at the inner struggle, the reader may additionally furthermore become bored.

Don't undergo in mind me? I endorse you watch and observe the collection Reprisal and the film Kill Bill. You also can have a look at my rant approximately the dearth of tale in Reprisal on my blog.

Reprisal modified into an captivating enough collection for me to take a look at each episode. Like Kill Bill, it's miles about a heroine that is left for lifeless through her circle of relatives and who returns to searching for revenge.

But the gathering finale left me questioning what the factor of all of that become. Why did they do what they did to Katherine Harlow? And why did she pass seeking out revenge anyhow those years? This inner war that drove her to make the motion isn't always particular in Reprisal. The sports are nice there to serve the plot:

Katherine arrives at a location and sees that her brother and some others have killed severa guys. She screams he didn't want to do it.

Now she is aware about what they did, and there may be a high-quality risk she'll inform the others. So the awful guys (of them being her very non-public husband and brother) chain her to the decrease lower returned of a pickup and drag her at some stage in the tarmac. They count on she is dead.

She returns years later and starts offevolved offevolved to are searching for revenge.

There are a chain of events. People kill every different. There are severa fights, masses of blood, and dramatic track.

The best reason the gathering gives to provide an explanation for why her brother killed the ones men is that they will be part of rival gangs, and he preferred struggle. What emerge as the reason of the struggle? Who is privy to!

Why emerge as her brother so cruel to drag her in the course of the asphalt? The display says that "she deserved more than a shotgun to the pinnacle." But what does this advise? Was she a bad character? Was a shotgun too common for her? The courting many of the siblings is never advanced enough for us to discover.

Why did the husband comply with kill his very non-public accomplice? Because Katherine's brother crammed his head with "mind of own family and big matters we have been going to do." What are these huge topics? What circle of relatives mind? Isn't his spouse part of his circle of relatives? What drove the husband to betray her like that? The courting among the two is in no manner advanced sufficient for us to discover.

The plot is critical to the tale, however if you do not create an impact on the characters, you threat leaving the reader frustrated which you wasted their time.

When you compare this tale to Kill Bill, you get some issue plenty greater memorable and impactful. The premise and the beginning are similar. Yet, within the film, it's far apparent the character wasn't happy collectively along with her existence as a killer. She favored to loosen up and characteristic a circle of relatives, especially for the reason that she end up pregnant. Her internal conflict modified into one in every of affection. She preferred to stay a peaceful life, freed from the nightmares she had endured.

AND BANG BANG!

Bill came alongside and took all that far from her. Why did he do all that? When we watch the movie, we see how near the characters are and the way betrayed he feels even as she leaves him. Why does she need revenge? Because Bill took away her threat to meet her greatest desire: to start a circle of relatives.

The man or woman's motivations and inner warfare are related to the tale's outdoor activities. This is because of the fact, at the same time as the outside hassle captures the reader, it is the internal hassle that makes the e-book memorable.

If you're a plotter (Chapter 3), you could hold plotting the story. But recall to reflect onconsideration on how an event will have an effect on your person. Consider what sort of internal struggle would in all likelihood stand up because of that occasion. If you're a pantser, you do not want to jot down about what is going to display up, however with every new concept, maintain in thoughts:

Why this takes region?

Whether it is relevant. Don't positioned scenes in the tale genuinely to fill pages. Each scene need to be crucial to increase the plot or be a part of the man or woman's emotional adventure.

Whether they assessment with each exclusive. Not the entirety wishes to be all conflict. And now not the entirety needs to seem fast or typically slowly. The remarkable memories captivate us due to their assessment. They deliver us time to respire, time to root for the person, grieve at their loss and have amusing at their victories.

A tale this is actually an outdoor event after an external occasion, or battle after battle, reads like a list of events. And a story wherein there can be no transformation is a tale that falls quick of what the reader expects. When you ask your self why some factor takes area, and the solution is:

A: Because it seems like something lousy that no person dreams for it to arise, so I'll positioned it there to make my reader undergo.

Q: Yes, however does it impact what happens subsequent? Does it affect the person because it forces her to stand her inner battle? If it's no longer part of the e-book, will it make a difference to the save you of the tale?

A: No, however it looks like some element awful that no person needs for it to expose up, so I'll positioned it there to make my reader go through.

Then you have were given a hassle on your e-book. The matters that appear should make enjoy in the end.

If you're a plotter, now can be the correct possibility to create an define of your tale. Create a chain of activities (plot) and scenes that allows you to fuel the internal battle (story) in your character. Make certain they are interconnected. And typically ask yourself: Why? Why is this occasion essential for my tale? If you are a pantser, make sure you furthermore may do this at some point of the writing technique.

Chapter 13: The Hook

If you examine lots, then you definately definately in reality must have have a have a look at a few organising sentences that intrigued you sufficient to make you want to hold analyzing. For example:

1.   "Alicia Berenson have become thirty-3 years vintage whilst she killed her husband" through Alex Michaelides, The Silent Patient.

2.   "Have you ever perplexed how lengthy it takes to dig a grave?" by using using Catherine Steadman, Something in the Water.

…are thrilling terms that hook you with the primary line.

So now that you want to put in writing your e-book, you discover your self questioning that if you do not have an first rate starting sentence, then no one will want to study the ebook. You decide to install writing a pleasing prologue revealing how movement-packed the ebook can be in truth to inspire readers to hold on the second one web page. Or you turn your foremost man or woman's existence the other way up at the first actual internet web page and count on it to surprise or surprise the reader.

Who can relate? Can I positioned my hand up when I'm the only giving the recommendation?

What if I instructed you that you do now not want an top notch sentence?

Obviously, if you could write a catchy sentence like:

three. "It changed into a vibrant bloodless day in April, and the clocks were putting 13." The beginning sentence of George Orwell's 1984, or

4. "As Gregor Samsa awoke one morning from uneasy goals he decided himself transformed in his bed right into a remarkable insect." Like Franz Kafka in The Metamorphosis.

...even higher.

However, no longer all books can obtain a enjoy of intrigue with out revealing too much or leaping to the wrong section. And, in my opinion, some of the hole sentences that have been branded as some of the great are not that compelling. They have simplest emerge as broadly recognized because of the e-book's achievement.

A suitable starting off sentence need to have a sure element of intrigue, yes, if you can. But try and supply away some aspect particular approximately your fundamental individual or the area you've got created. Above all, ensure the primary sentence is nicely-written and paced absolutely so it's far a outstanding starting up.

But at the same time as we communicate approximately hooks, we aren't talking approximately commencing sentences. What you want to consciousness on is the hook that draws readers in to observe the subsequent bankruptcy. Which might not imply turning the principle character's lifestyles the alternative way up on the primary net web page.

Think of all the books wherein the characters lose their parents early within the ebook. The form of instances a love triangle has been used. Or even those wherein characters face the stop of the area. Did you care about those testimonies in addition? Have you saved studying until 3 in the morning each ebook you have got ever picked up? No? Probably due to the truth the author did now not create a hook that have become interesting or impactful enough for you.

The hook is what attracts the reader to the internet web page. It's the person's internal struggle that explains why we need to feel empathy for this fictional being. This method that it's miles the inner battle that entices the reader to examine the primary sentence, first paragraph, or first bankruptcy.

When we have a look at the primary sentence of The Hunger Games with the aid of way of Suzanne Collins:

5. "When I wake up, the possibility component of the mattress is bloodless. My hands stretch out, trying to find Prim's warmth however locating simplest the hard canvas cover of the mattress."

We do no longer reflect onconsideration on this as a lovely sentence. However, the subsequent sentence:

"She need to have had horrific desires and climbed in with our mother. Of route, she did. This is the day of the reaping."

Already puzzles us a touch more. We marvel why a few issue like a reaping day ought to deliver someone nightmares. But we brush aside the word because of the truth we are talking about small children. They have nightmares and search for their mothers in the direction of the night time time.

It isn't always this sentence that grabs us. However, the primary bankruptcy is filled with inner struggle. Katniss goes into the wooded region, and we commonly have that word, the reaping, soaring like it's far a swear phrase. We discover Katniss's global as being a risky region. We comprehend she is someone creative who has misplaced her father and stays now not dealing with it thoroughly. Gale appears, and we discover that Katniss harbors resentment closer to her mom and that she faces chance due to the fact she feels a responsibility to take care of her circle of relatives. Gale exhibits Katniss' internal conflict as they speak approximately the possibility of leaving collectively. She wouldn't be able to due to the fact she cares for her sister mainly else. Her aim is to defend her sister. We additionally analyze the which means of the reaping. So, while the ultimate internet net page of the bankruptcy arrives and Katniss' sister's call, Prim, comes out in the reaping, we can not help however sense intrigued approximately what takes area subsequent.

When we have a look at an interesting story that speaks to our unconscious, we emerge as part of that global. We see the arena the same manner the characters do. This is because, inside the maximum primitive of tactics, reminiscences permit us to help interpret and expect our reactions and those of others. When we hook up with the character, we cannot help however assume: how can also I react in this case?

This is why setting up the inner struggle in someone is so important. The plot is essential to convey out the internal battle, but it's far the war that makes the reader connect with the person.

This is why it's miles Prim's name that comes out within the reaping in preference to Katniss's. Suzanne Collins may also additionally need to have thoroughly decided to expose Katniss' call and pressure her to compete in the Hunger Games besides. The reader can also have concept, "Wow! Tough good fortune." However, Katniss' critical motivation is set up early within the story: she wishes to protect her sister. Katniss isn't a person to whom some thing horrible occurs.

She is a person who deserves empathy due to the fact that a few thing horrible is important to the character's development we examine inside the narrative.

If the financial break had began with the reaping, ought to what takes location to the Everdeen own family be awful? Of path! Would it have the equal effect? Would it grow to be the phenomenon it's miles in recent times? Maybe positive, or possibly not. We do no longer know Katniss well enough to understand how a whole lot she cares for her sister, so the reader wouldn't care each.

In the primary financial disaster, for your hook, you need to provide the reader a motive to care. To do that, before you supply him a motivation, a cause, or preference—something he's going to pursue due to the fact the trouble of the story (external event)—you want to offer him a flaw, a worry he needs to overcome, or a lesson he wants to have a study (internal trouble).

How do you try this?

By displaying "Day 1" in the lifestyles of your person.

Their lifestyles earlier than the inciting incident alters his trajectory. "Day 1" is only a concept; it does no longer want to be the day earlier than the triggering event. But even on the primary day, you need to expose some warfare. What the man or woman dreams, or how their existence is defective because of a lesson they must study. However, on that first day, inside the existence earlier than the out of doors event adjustments the heroine's direction, you want to expose how their fear or flaw is affecting the protagonist's life. This is because of the truth your man or woman does not exist from the instantaneous a few detail extreme or traumatic takes area. They had been already someone with a beyond, with goals and fears earlier than the number one net web page. You need to make that seen.

The internal warfare is the method among some thing your person desires and the concern that stops them from conducting it.

INTERNAL CONFLICT = DESIRE vs. FEAR

All tales are approximately transformation: first-rate adjustments (exceptional arc), bad versions (poor arc), or a person looking at the transformation of others (flat arc). I will communicate greater approximately those in a while. We aren't inquisitive about following the lifestyles of someone who transforms if we do no longer comprehend how they commenced out.

When I began writing Sombras (Shadows), I turn out to be at a downside because of the truth, unlike you, who simply take a look at the ones pages, I failed to recognize this components. However, there are although subjects we recognise approximately Lilly in the first financial ruin:

1. Lilly has a first-rate lifestyles, however she feels something is lacking. Yet, she we

should herself go at the bandwagon due to the fact each person tells her how perfect her existence is.

2.   Lilly desires to do something impulsive.

Lilly's internal war is looking to be more impulsive (preference) however feeling frightened of disappointing others (worry). In her case, while now not having to reveal herself to her own family, she may be able to go after her desire and bounce in headfirst. Things get complex at the same time as the individual gives in to vintage behavior: searching for to delight others, or even as what she desired for, to be impulsive, brings her dire outcomes. Anyway, even at its maximum primary degree, warfare and plot are continuously intertwined.

And it is this war so that it will make the tale flow into in advance and make the reader stay in conjunction with your man or woman.

Why?

Because of empathy.

Lisa Cron gives a logical purpose of why we fall in love with recollections in her ebook Story Genius. We are all fearful of pain, so we look at books to have a have a look at others experience it. Not due to the fact we are masochists but due to the reality this commentary teaches us the manner to stand the world. We might not all experience empathy in the conflict among human beings and killer robots, however all of us have goals, and anybody, in our lives, have had some element stopping us from pursuing those dreams. The character's stop purpose may not be the same as the reader's, however you'll feel empathy for a person who faces their fears and grows as a quit result. Because books train us a way to navigate our way thru lifestyles.

Start via considering the why of the tale you need to write. Is there something you want to explore? Some message? Maybe this is your battle. Whatever your first chapter (your hook) is, you've got got were given to show it in a few manner. Think:

1- What your protagonist thinks will deliver them happiness.

2- What fear prevents them from accomplishing their desire?

When the inciting incident takes place (the outside problem), the hero of your tale will haven't any desire however to embark on the inner adventure, despite the fact that they don't understand it.

Almost every e book, whether or not or now not movement, romance, or horror, has a hidden lesson. The internal journey is not obvious, but that is what resonates with the reader. And that's what makes awesome reminiscences greater memorable than others.

Chapter 14: The Inciting Incident

Now that I've long lengthy long gone on and on approximately how important it is to present your primary character a preference and a fear and cause them to research a lesson, you are probably thinking that is all there can be to a tale. You may additionally marvel, "How can I in shape flying automobiles, shooting, and heartbreaking romance if I'm presupposed to popularity on their internal adventure?" Don't worry. You can although have an motion-packed e-book and feature your hero observe some difficulty.

Ready Player One with the useful resource of Ernest Cline is a generation fantasy e-book about a virtual international. Because it's far movement-packed, it is able to not be apparent to everybody that it also has a message. The e-book tells us to not be afraid to stay inside the real worldwide. Jane Austen's Pride and Prejudice is a conventional novel approximately romance, but the crucial characters can most effective be collectively after overcoming their pleasure and their prejudice. Vampire Academy with the aid of Richelle Mead is a myth novel about vampires in a college, but it additionally explores the topics of friendship and responsibility.

We can also moreover need to all enhance our lives with the resource of reading a lesson or . We moreover have desires and desires that we do no longer pursue due to our fears. We recognize that exchange can deliver benefits, but the biology of people is made to face up to alternate. However, the inciting incident is one an wonderful way to catapult your protagonist's life, whether or now not or now not they need it.

It's the component at which the man or woman is pushed into what will be the start of the plot manufacturing, e.G., training dragons or stopping children to the demise. The "call to journey," as Joseph Campbell puts it in The Hero's Journey. This occasion will regulate the character's life and generate all kinds of adventures, courses, and internal adjustments so one can allow the improvement of an concerning and addictive narrative.

Take, for instance, a person who wants to find lasting love however does now not apprehend because of the truth he's spent his entire life combating in opposition to it out of worry of being damage. His thoughts makes 1000-and-one excuses to live unmarried or stay a womanizer. He secretly goals a connection, however there may be some trouble in his past that has made him trust that love does no longer exist or that love brings more ache than happiness. This is the false impression of the area or lies your person believes in. Your inciting incident will change that. The hassle is that, until now, your man or woman in no manner left his consolation vicinity, and he glad himself that he had the entirety he had to be happy, so they'll fight in opposition to that trade. So whether or not or now not it's a brand new love, a little one, a pup, or a terminal illness, you will placed some factor in the front of him as a manner to reveal his lifestyles the wrong way up and reason doubt to creep in.

In Abbie Emmons' motion pix, she states really what second to your story you ought to introduce the inciting incident. It's whilst the man or woman's existence comes down to 2 picks:

a) Continue in their comfort vicinity and in no way get what they need.

b) Accept the choice to journey, carry out a bit problem unique and face the unknown at the same time as continuing to keep away from his fear.

This part of persevering with to keep away from his worry is important for the continuation of your narrative. It creates the usaand downs that make your ebook have a look at glaringly.

The element of the inciting incident is to pressure the character to stand a exchange in their lives. However, their flaws will generally be there, developing limitations.

Will Freeman (Once Upon a Boy by way of using manner of Nick Hornby) failed to meet Marcus and assume, "Now I want to be responsible and a tremendous have an effect on." He spent many turning elements within the narrative doing matters the wrong manner till he discovered his lesson. Similarly, a womanizer does now not discover he has a terminal infection and says, "Wow! Now I need to get married." He will keep to persuade himself that the existence he has led so far makes him satisfied. Your interest can be to region barriers inside the front of his route that make him mirror. Maybe he's going to ought to go to treatments on my own and sees a couple managing the sickness as partners. Maybe he's going to visit his satisfactory buddy's son's baptism and enjoy a touch of jealousy for what he is going to in no manner have. The possibilities are infinite.

Tips for creating an inciting incident:

Connect the event with the primary storyline

When I say to attach the 2, I do not mean that due to the fact you write about aliens, your inciting incident desires to be about aliens. What I suggest is it need to be obvious the protagonist went to combat the aliens due to the reality some issue in the event set him on the course to meet them. Katniss takes element in the Hunger Games because of the fact her sister's call got here up inside the reaping in the course of her occasion, which made her volunteer. Ender is recruited to the Battle School in Orson Scott Card's The End Game due to his prowess in combating the bullies who attacked him in his inciting incident.

Stay on the identical timeline

If your inciting incident passed off inside the past and you've were given the person casually are searching for for recommendation from it, you take away the opportunity for the reader to revel in it with the man or woman. We are with Starr in Angie Thomas's novel The Hate U Give while she loses a pal on the fingers of the police. In Gone Girl via Gillian Flynn, we see Nick come domestic and understand his companion has vanished. In A Christmas Carol via Charles Dickens, we are visited by using way of the use of Marley's ghost, at the component of Scrooge, who warns him approximately the 3 ghosts as a way to preserve-out him.

It must be something that remains with you for the relaxation of the tale

Your instigating occasion can't be resolved right away in a single motion. If you solve the war at the number one web page, your man or woman not has to pursue their motivation or remedy the trouble that introduced them into the movement. A tale is a mixture of smaller troubles to remedy a massive problem. A correlation of purpose and impact. The outcome that comes out of your protagonist fixing one hassle ought to have a proper away impact on the following one. After witnessing his buddy's homicide, Starr makes a choice to intervene via the use of coming in advance as a witness (The Hate U Give). The police, however, refuse to arrest the officer she identifies. The number one difficulty, getting justice for her pal's loss of life, isn't solved in a unmarried movement. Nick embarks on a turbulent journey to discover his spouse, but the event not nice does now not solve itself in a single motion however additionally casts him as a suspect (Gone Girl).

The individual will have to evolve

Most humans do not alternate till they are compelled to by way of manner of an unavoidable outside. The inciting incident is the fuse for that evolution. It is the event if you want to create some other chain of activities and stress the character out in their comfort area. What takes vicinity at the same time as human beings determine to step out in their comfort zone? They evolve. For better or for worse. In Gone Girl, Nick shows on the adjustments in his courting and asks himself, "Who are you? What have we completed to every one-of-a-kind? What are we going to do?" As the tale progresses, we see Nick gain the courage to confront his spouse, despite the fact that one final task makes matters greater complex. Despite this, the person has in spite of the fact that grown and now has the solutions to the questions he requested himself at the start.

Chapter 15: Three Act Structure

Every new author starts with the preference to inform a notable tale. However, masses folks are intimidated with the useful resource of the usage of the complexity required to create a hundred-three hundred-net web page e-book. We fear we might not have sufficient cloth to tell a tale, and we will end up with a e-book entire of terms that lead us nowhere.

That is why, earlier than you start writing, you want to come to be acquainted with how tale form works. If an awesome plot is needed to lure a reader to choose out up a e book and internal struggle is the essential element to developing memorable characters, then tale form is the formulation that binds each elements together. Structure presents the framework for the story, permitting it to move from one plot Point to the following while making sure that every factor serves a particular cause. It is what movements the plot earlier and connects the character's inner journey to the outside sports on the way to expose up in parallel at particular moments within the story.

One of the most well-known formulas in literature and movie is the three Act Structure. And no ebook (that I understand of) explains this shape better than Jessica Brody's Save the Cat! Writes a Novel.

This technique is based totally totally on the premise that each tale has three elements: the beginning, the middle, and the cease. Each of these three acts is in addition subdivided into subcategories that assist the author enlarge the character's journey, their arc, and the story's plot.

Some writers are in competition to the use of the approach for worry that the story will seem too formulaic. However, the approach is handiest a shape to boom the key moments of the tale.

The three-act form can be systematized, as supplied in Figure 1:

Act One — The Presentation

The motion starts inside the first act, the beginning of our tale. It is proper right here which you need to introduce your protagonist, the hero of the story, to the reader. And, as we've already explored, the heroine want to be someone who has lived a normal lifestyles thus far. Even if that lifestyles modified into horrible, with all of the possible and no longer feasible troubles, it modified into everyday for her.

In this section, you can set the scene for the readers and offer an reason behind who your man or woman is, what an afternoon inside the lifestyles of this individual is like, the area they live in, their relationships, and their goals (hook). Because if the reader does not understand the essence of the hero, they may no longer be capable of apprehend the transformation or the lesson the hero will research.

The habitual lifestyles of the individual is probably disturbed by using hook or through crook (the inciting incident), and topics trade.

The 2nd arrives while your hero may be pressured to make a desire: each neglect approximately what has passed off and go back to his regular life or take delivery of the selection to adventure and float in advance.

This choice will cause doubts.

It is a large choice to be taken gently. The inciting incident must be something that modifications the direction of the hero's life and creates a few inner conflict. This is due to the fact, until now, the individual has felt secure in his comfort area. It is perfectly natural to experience doubts and to ponder on the subsequent step. To think whether he is going to make the selection in order to redecorate his lifestyles. And this is wherein you could furthermore range a touch:

a) In the primary opportunity, you can make the protagonist forget approximately approximately the selection to journey and flow decrease lower back to her regular life. However, you'll keep to throw conflicts that permits you to force the protagonist to truely receive the decision afterward.

b) In the second alternative, the inciting incident and the doubts display up nearly simultaneously. The protagonist ought to now not have plenty time to make the choice.

In the end, the stop end result is the identical. The protagonist accepts the choice, and as quick as the selection is made, there may be no turning another time. We enter the primary turning point.

Act One Example

Using the example of The Hunger Games, as in the preceding chapter, permit's discover how the story develops the usage of this shape. If you have not examine the ebook but, I want to offer you with a warning that there are spoilers (and masses of them).

Hook: the day of the reaping. Katniss is furnished as someone who in reality wants to live to tell the tale and is scared of the Capital. Her stated choice is to keep her sister secure.

Inciting incident: the call of Katniss' sister, Prim, is selected for the Hunger Games.

Doubt: Katniss does now not have lots time to make a preference, so she accepts the choice to journey and volunteers for the games.

Act Two — The Confrontation

Your man or woman has made the proper preference in answering the call to adventure. However, not something is probably clean. Otherwise, the tale might be over earlier than it even began out. In the second act, you may have to expose how a good buy the heroine's lifestyles will change through accepting the choice.

The hero has determined to get what he thinks may carry him happiness or has selected the direction that could reason him a whole lot less pain. Either way, the motive is the pursuit of happiness and fending off the concern we've set in the direction of the hook. Your intention as a author may be to place boundaries inside the hero's direction, whether or not as existence problems or detrimental forces. How many? That is sincerely up to you; it's miles your story. Just make sure you hold the narrative interesting. Include factors of surprise, adventure, and twists and turns. But do no longer weigh down the reader through collectively with the whole lot right away. The notable memories are those who've quiet moments interspersed that permit the reader some time to respire.

The fundamental mission inside the first a part of the second one act is that, regardless of having often going on the selection to adventure, the hero's remedy is probably tested as she reacts to limitations (we call this the reactionary hero). The hero has but to have a look at the lesson or conquer the concern we cited within the first act. Because of this, she will are searching out to clear up problems or challenges within the wrong manner.

Midpoint

Something massive will seem inside the center of the ebook so one can be a turning element in your story. You can call it a midpoint or a plot twist. But like I said, the heroine hasn't found out her lesson but, and as a result, she's been solving problems the wrong manner. Maybe the entirety has worked up to date, but she realizes she is still unhappy. Or, due to her normal errors, she realizes her moves were an entire failure. Something massive will take place. It might be a wedding idea in which the heroine, who has been proud and prejudiced until now, realizes how pathetic her love life has been because of her flaws (Jane Austen's Pride and Prejudice). Or perhaps she's been displaying her new boss how she might be capable of live to the fullest but remains caught collectively with her antique boyfriend who does no longer recognize her (Me Before You thru Jojo Moyes).

Whatever it's far, he realizes till he modifications strategies, he can not gain the happiness he seeks. He is in the long run prepared to investigate his lesson or face his worry. We skip from reactionary hero to active hero.

Now that the hero has modified his mindset, the second one a part of the second one act will show the hero's taking motion in the direction of the damaging forces. The second element carries a chain of events (or barriers) that show the hero's perseverance and the way the game has modified.

However, the antagonist forces hold to deliver the hero down thru using destroying relationships, dropping jobs, with bosses with goals of euthanasia (Me Before You), or greater more youthful sisters who decide to run away with soldiers (Pride and Prejudice). Just due to the fact the hero is prepared to genuinely obtain the lesson he wishes to investigate, a modern-day disaster movements. This new obstacle is greater than all of the others confronted and leads the hero to lose the self notion he has received so far. It is also at this component that the hero has no choice however to surely be for the reason that he has been fending off handling his worry.

Act Two Example

At the surrender of Act 1, Katniss has agreed to sign up inside the Hunger Games and have to make the journey to the Capital, which she despises.

Reactionary Heroine: Katniss does no longer actively fight (does not act) in competition to the restrictions thrown at her within the Capital. She accepts the policies to live alive and handiest reacts to the limits. Even even as the games start, her intuition is to stay to inform the story, it is why she runs away.

Midpoint: After finding herself among a rock and a tough region, Katniss exhibits herself on pinnacle of a tree and no longer the usage of a way out. She is privy to she has no distinctive preference. To live to tell the story, she should start gambling the video games and kill.

Twist: This choice is the catalyst for what follows. Katniss office work an alliance with Rue and decides to assault the alternative game enthusiasts' reserves. She stops being a reactionary hero and goes at the offensive.

Disaster: Despite Katniss' newfound willpower, on the save you of the second one act, she suffers a vast loss, Rue's lack of life.

Crisis: Despite her promise to Rue, Katniss feels doubt. She keeps considering Peeta and the boy she killed.

At the climax of Act Two, they announce that there can be winners if they will be from the identical district. The search for Peeta starts offevolved.

Act Three — The Resolution

It is proper right here, all over again, that the plot and the transformational adventure of the hero come collectively. Act 3 ought to reveal how a outstanding deal the protagonist has modified because of the out of doors events of the previous acts. The heroine can board the aircraft to mention goodbye to the person she loves and strive once more to persuade him to change his mind, accepting the state of affairs even as she fails (Me Before You). Alternatively, the heroine realizes her prejudice has once more interfered collectively along with her love existence and resolves to be happy thru accepting the marriage notion from the man or woman she loves (Pride and Prejudice).

The 1/three act may additionally variety in how linear it's far:

a) The hero admits his worry and accepts that if he does no longer combat, he might also lose the entirety he has fought for up to now. This may be a literal warfare or a love hobby, or it could be a last operation closer to a sickness or a few special adversarial stress.

b) What took place on the surrender of the second one act changed into so devastating that it destroyed the hero's hopes and desires. The hero loses his morale and is prepared to give up the adventure. Suddenly, as he is ready to surrender, a person gives him the rush he so desperately goals. They make him recognize that if he offers up now, it will all be in useless. The hero regains his composure and musters the braveness to confront the antagonist and his worry.

Whether you select choice "a" or "b" within the third act, the climax need to be the aspect with the maximum anxiety inside the story. This is the element at which the character has the whole lot to lose or gain. The purpose so that it will deliver her happiness is on the alternative aspect, and the reader need to experience the same manner. Whatever the very last effects, make sure the hero profits a few issue from the struggle, whether or no longer it's a lesson, an answer, or the belief that the cause she desired to advantage changed into not constantly the one she become aiming for. Connect the resolution with the precept state of affairs rely of the story: the lesson you want to hold to the reader.

It is the message of your tale at the way to stay with the reader prolonged after the ebook is finished.

In the surrender, all you've got had been given left to do is show the reader the hero's life after the transformation or hint that extra adventures will come.

Act Three Example

Katniss keeps to suppress the trauma of her past and present to keep to live on. She furthermore keeps to deny her emotions for Peeta, convincing herself that the notable cause she went seeking out him turn out to be in order that she must live to inform the story. But when they announce that what all of the tributes require can be in the middle of the area, Katniss does now not hesitate—she desires to shop Peeta. Otherwise, he may additionally moreover die. Katniss dangers her life for Peeta and has to admit that she may additionally now not be really surviving.

In the final conflict, Katniss and Peeta combat Cato. And they assume they have obtained the video games. At this 2d, Katniss learns what she's been retaining off. She would not absolutely need to live to inform the tale. She wants to stay on her phrases and with dignity. By managing her fear, the Capitol, she commits her first act of defiance on the identical time as she threatens to devour the toxic berries with Peeta.

The story ends with every Katniss and Peeta as winners. She is now not just a woman who desires to live to tell the story. She has end up a photograph of desire.

You might imagine, what if I want to write down down multiple e-book?

The answer is easy: whether there are three or seven books, they need to conform with a comparable form to the three acts even as blended. If you're thinking about writing a trilogy, have a look at some aspect like this:

Book 1 - Act 1

Book 2 - Act 2

Book three - Act three

Each man or woman ebook need to have its personal journey of transformation and its personal shape. The stakes end up better with every new ebook and bring about a lesson that pertains to the massive last lesson.

A very a fulfillment example of this is the Harry Potter books. Each ebook has its personal theme, and with every passing year, Harry desires to investigate some component about himself in case you want to permit him to defeat Voldemort.

1. In the number one ebook, the subject of the story is love. The truth that Lily gave her lifestyles for Harry's have end up him into the "boy who lived."

2. In the second one ebook, the subject is prejudice. A massive basilisk assaults best the students of a positive bloodline.

3. The difficulty consider of the 0.33 ebook is braveness and loyalty. The e-book is dedicated to Harry's combat in competition to the dementors and the loyalty of Harry's mother and father' pals.

4. The fourth e-book is prepared tolerance. Through the Tournament of Three Wizards, Harry learns to just accept the traits of people he previously judged, and Hermione starts offevolved offevolved the club inside the path of the mistreatment of elves.

five. The fifth e-book is ready friendship and fate. Harry isolates himself, and a prophecy about him comes out. In the end, he's conscious that his future connects him to Voldemort, however he differs from him thanks to the love of his friends.

6. The sixth e-book is ready confronting the beyond. The tale leads us to find out Voldemort's beyond as Harry involves terms alongside together together with his private.

7. The task count of the seventh and very last e-book is sacrifice. And it is this ultimate lesson that enables Harry defeat Voldemort.

All the books are intertwined with an everyday subject remember, the recognition of the stability amongst existence and loss of lifestyles, which permits Harry expand as a hero.

Chapter 16: Description

Description is one of the most vital components of a e book. It's what enables the reader visualizes the placing throughout the tale. The tale becomes hollow without description because of the truth it's far only activities being suggested. The reader's creativeness cannot evoke the senses if it has no foundation. The important assignment with description is to balance what's too much—plenty descriptive facts that bores the reader—and what is too little that the reader lacks sufficient element to revel in gift within the story.

"Sentences want to respire, unfastened from more verbiage. A well-decided on noun, a mot juste, is well virtually worth greater than a list of attributes."

João de Mancelos

Not all readers much like the equal quantity of detail. Some love and have fun with all the information they get approximately the individual's worldwide, on the same time as others can't stand descriptive scenes. It's up to you, as the writer, to decide what you need your reader to visualize and what you need to go away to the creativeness.

Again, this is additionally a few element that gets higher with enjoy. When I started writing Sombras (Shadows), I dreaded descriptions (and to be honest, I nonetheless do). Long descriptions in books have in no manner appealed to me as a reader, and when I encounter one, I discover myself disconnecting from the story or skipping the net web page. When I first started out out writing, I knew it'd be my worst nightmare because of the fact if studying loads is a creator's first tool, then how can you sharpen that tool if your thoughts does not popularity during the descriptive elements?

If I can get a few compliments on my capability to assemble brilliant descriptions, then so are you capable of! The trick is to recognize what your susceptible factors are as a creator and positioned double the attempt into the ones elements. Over time, workout will assist you enhance. As a reader and creator, I've placed that during case you spread the facts out over the scene and produce the point of interest again to the man or woman, you may frequently break out with some facts, particularly if you write YA.

If, like me, you moreover mght do not like descriptions the least bit, my advice is to keep away from them inside the first draft. Your first draft need to be the fun a part of the technique even as you find out your tale and collect the characters. If you want to perform a little element you do not like proper at the start, then you can procrastinate until the final 2nd, and you may bypass over that connection with the story. I now not regularly encompass descriptions in my first draft, other than one element or every other that jumps to thoughts. I quality recognition at the statistics at some degree inside the 2nd one draft.

I start via the use of visualizing the scenario I need to offer an cause of and searching the net for pics to assist me discover it. I describe what I see within the pix and encompass what I don't forget feeling, paying attention to, or smelling in that state of affairs. I moreover seek the net for key phrases which can describe those sounds and smells.

I in no way embody all the senses in the description. This can add up to two or 3 paragraphs of description and end up too uninteresting. So, my very last step is to investigate descriptions made with the aid of manner of diverse writers and have a examine how they make description and narration intertwine.

What I regularly test is that the trick is to in no manner deliver the whole description proper away. I encompass a sentence or two of description, then I deliver the eye again to the intrigue or the man or woman's mind, encompass every other element of description, then communicate or a latest second of narration.

Richie heard snarling sounds. They were very loud—the sounds a wild animal in a cage might also additionally make. He located loafers descend the stairs. Faded jeans on top of them—swinging palms—

But they weren't hands . . . They had been paws. Huge, misshapen paws.

"Cuh-cuh-climb the c-c-coal!" Bill became screaming, but Richie stood frozen, knowing what grow to be coming for them, what turn out to be going to kill them on this cellar that stank of damp earth and the cheap wine that had been spilled in the corners. Knowing but looking to see. "There's a wuh-wuh-window at the t-top of the c-coal!"

The paws had been included with dense brown hair that curled and coiled like wire; the hands have been tipped with jagged nails. Now Richie noticed a silk jacket. It turn out to be black with orange piping—the Derry High School colorings.

Stephen King, IT: Book 1

You can inform from this excerpt that the characters have heard sounds that sound like wild animals, that they will be in a cellar that smells like damp and spilled wine, that they may be terrified, and what the creature that frightens them looks as if. This records, but, wasn't furnished to the reader suddenly, giving them time to breathe and end up immersed within the story. The description is finished sequentially and interspersed with the narration, related to the reader in discovering not fine the activities however moreover the placing of the motion, in addition to the traits and feelings of the characters.

Exercise: Think about your favorite location. How can also need to you describe it to a person who has by no means been there? How special is this vicinity for you?

Chapter 17: Show, Don't Tell

Show, do not inform is an immersion technique in which the story is defined through movements and sensory information in preference to exposition. It is a manner used to seize the reader's hobby by using using their private research and emotions.

One example most usually used by writers to offer an reason for the difference amongst them—you could see it used by Stephen King, João de Mancelos, and on the weblog, Reedsy—is from the Russian creator Anton Chekhov: "Don't inform me the moon is shining. Show me the glint of moderate on broken glass."

A creator who tells will honestly country that the moon have become shining. A author who suggests will tricky at the moon's reflection at the glass. Using this immersion method, the reader will recall a situation the use of deduction and linking their experience and information of the moon's shine and their reminiscence of broken glass.

Example

Mary changed into indignant.

vs.

Mary clenched her tooth and fists at the same time. Her nostrils had widened to the factor wherein she must nearly suit marbles inner.

We don't want the writer to tell us Mary became irritated. Angry humans will be predisposed to clench their enamel or make a fist. Sometimes every. We moreover understand that our nostrils get barely enlarged at the same time as enraged. Because of our very personal revel in, we're capable of envision the scenario and Mary's very very own feelings.

How often were you disappointed after making plans a surprise which you had been positive the recipient may also experience, fine to have them say they desired it, however you did no longer sense like they did? The terms permit you to know what you expected to pay interest, but the emotions do now not. That is the essence of showing in desire to telling.

A reader can be disillusioned in the event that they most effective examine the words on paper and can't enjoy what the story is trying to deliver. The purpose proper right here is to immerse them within the studying enjoy and lead them to miss they are analyzing a few difficulty fictional.

Example

John walked into the room and felt at domestic over again.

vs.

As fast as he walked into the room, the crackle of the fireplace and the fragrance of eucalyptus invaded his senses and embraced him. He discovered his grandfather's vintage rocking chair, his grandmother's knitting needles, and his father's cluttered table. The fairly spiced aroma of his mom's cottage pie brought lower returned reminiscences that made him enjoy warm and energized.

Which of these terms makes you sense fuzzy and cushty?

You do now not need to mix fragrance, sight, touch, paying attention to, and taste all inside the identical sentence. Try to interrupt up them at the same time as you convey the reader into the same room because the man or woman. Make them scent, see, and sense what you're describing.

Close your eyes and visualize the scene you need the reader to appearance. What do you take a look at? Woods, seashores, or flatlands? What are you smelling? Perhaps it's lunchtime at some stage in the summer season. Do the streets fragrance like roasted sardines or meat on the grill? Or probably it is a winter's night time, and also you experience the easy air and a faint scent of burning pine? What do you enjoy? The solar warming your pores and skin, sweat pouring down your face? Is the bloodless freezing your ears and chapping your lips? What do you concentrate? Fireworks? The waves on the seaside? Leaves rustling and dancing? The sound of the wind on the thirty-first floor?

According to a fellow writer, the primary English model of my quick tale, The Banshee Cries—which changed into then referred to as The Roommate on the time—became very descriptive. I saved telling the reader what passed off as opposed to letting them discern it out for themselves. Years later, I rewrote the tale and attempted to depict the putting and sports activities in a contemporary mild. Another author pal have a study my ebook and admitted to feeling scared in a few factors. I had created an image with loads tension that it had via some way surpassed my non-public expectations and caused the reader to experience intrigued.

This changed into nice possible due to my efforts to decorate my method to show greater in desire to telling. Instead of pronouncing that the story has a dark tone, readers will recognize it because of the expressive sources of the language you operate.

Example

1. I first described the vicinity as an area that did no longer encourage agree with.

I actually have a weird feeling about this. I revel in as despite the fact that there may be a few aspect dark creeping inside the cracks among the rocks. Some poor or evil power if that have become a actual trouble.

2. I then interspersed moments of dialogue with moments of anxiety in my man or woman's inner communicate.

"Why do you watched she might be mourning in a place like this?" I ask.

"I don't understand her thoroughly. We most effective have a category collectively and she or he typically appeared a hint bit stuck as plenty as me." Motive? Check. I stroll slowly at the back of him and look for some issue I can use for safety. I spot a big sufficient rock and seize it from the floor. He has a crowbar…It appears handiest honest. "And she has a few nerve!"

I stumble upon a touch of anger and tighten my hands across the rock.

"What do you suggest?"

He hesitates. "It's nothing. We need to preserve moving."

three. By the time it reaches the climax of the anxiety, the reader is already worried within the story due to the fact they have got felt Melissa's man or woman's worry growing.

There changed into no want to tell the reader that Melissa emerge as afraid; the emotion is seen in her movements and thoughts. Nobody thinks, "I'm scared." We assume: "Oh, my goodness, someone is in our house" or "Damn! I come to be almost run over " Or "Shoot! Need to find a few thing to shield myself due to the fact I don't acquire as real with this guy." The mixture amongst talk and outline additionally offers anxiety and suspense.

This method fosters a more potent reference to the characters because of the fact we all revel in feelings in any other manner. You can write that Daisy become unhappy and Johanna have become unhappy. However, for Daisy, being unhappy way mendacity at the ground at the facet of her face swollen and thick tears streaming down her red face even as she makes a guttural sound. For Johanna, being unhappy method tightly clutching the couch cushion while staring into the emptiness and silently sobbing.

The feeling is the same, but the reactions of the characters range. And the situation you create and the volume of detail you provide will have an effect on what the reader is familiar with of every character's response.

In this way, displaying, in place of telling, permits us to get to recognise the characters in a deeper manner with the useful aid of seeing them have interaction with the world.

Instead of announcing a character is lazy, display him inert on the equal time because the people spherical him work. Show an unwillingness to cooperate whilst others ask him for assist. The greater you could get into your reader's minds, the higher their enjoy may be.

Now it's your flip:

Show that someone is irritated because of the way he talks to a person at a hotel reception.

Chapter 18: Dialogue

Dialogue refers to the section of a story text wherein conversations take location among characters. It is used to express the voice of the characters. If carried out nicely, it is one of the most critical gear the writer has at their disposal. It can force the development of the plot, create warfare and tension, and beautify the characterization of a individual through their personal feelings.

It is likewise one in each of my favored factors of a e-book. It's thru talk which you get to realize the real essence of the characters. It permits them to express their thoughts and feelings in their non-public terms and allows to bring them to existence. And I experience that it is thru the technique of dialogue that I installation "friendships" and begin to attend to a e-book's man or woman, making them seem greater "actual" to me.

The great talk is whilst the speech seems so natural that the writer's presence is on occasion vital. Good speak must sound like actual human beings speaking to each other, with appropriate pauses, fillers, and accents.

This is why you can often concentrate an writer advising you to be aware of real-existence conversations and teach your creator ear. I'm fine I've given this advice somewhere too. But after following that advice for a while, I found out that people rarely have conversations which might be well worth being transcribed right right into a e-book. Of direction, there are exceptions. And if you trap your buddies gossiping and also you take into account their memories are fraught with tension and battle, then it might be virtually properly well worth taking note of.

However, maximum of the verbal exchange you pay attention is small speak about work, our every day lives, and the climate. Avoid this section of the talk and proper now bounce to the best detail. Because correct speak have to make a reader enjoy like they will be eavesdropping on exclusive human beings's communication, however on an exquisite communique.

Avoid enriching the characters' vocabulary in reality so you can show off your literary talents. If your characters are 16-yr-vintage teenagers, they should now not talk as despite the fact that they have got swallowed a dictionary. As with most of the characters within the books of the Mortal Instruments series.

"Demons," drawled the blond boy, tracing the phrase on the air along together with his finger. "Religiously described as hell's denizens, the servants of Satan, but understood right right right here, for the capabilities of the Clave, to be any malevolent spirit whose starting area is out of doors our very private domestic size—"

Cassandra Clare, The City of Bones

I spent pretty some years not information why I couldn't connect with a e-book that quite an entire lot had the identical plot as mine and included all the factors that want to make it my favored book. After choosing it up again a few years later to look if I ought to deliver it another attempt, I placed out it was the communicate that made my eyes roll. Although I experience the story, the communicate makes me want to choke the characters. This can be an unpopular opinion—and the whole thing in writing and studying is subjective—however I feel that the speak in these books may want to no longer sound natural. All the characters speak in an unlikable, over-cultured way and attempt to make the equal jokes.

As I stated, it is within the talk that the characters ought to distinguish themselves so that the reader can installation "friendships" with them. So regardless of the fact that I locate the storyline thrilling, I can't seem to shape attachments to the characters.

As a long manner as speak is going, when you have a teenager who's genuinely versed, make certain you're making that a characteristic of that individual and keep away from repeating it for anybody else. If you have got someone who's normally cracking horrible jokes and by no means takes some thing appreciably, then do no longer repeat it for virtually all of us else. And drastically, avoid heavy sentences and monologues.

I observe someplace that normal humans do now not communicate in chunks of five sentences, contrary to what you may see in Grey's Anatomy. I by no means discovered if it's miles a few factor that truely happens in the display or not, but it is some thing I try and keep away from. The writer must chorus from the use of greater than twenty-5 terms in each sentence.

If you have got a person speakme for a long time, attempt to shift among the narration and the define of the alternative characters' reactions, regardless of the fact that they sincerely use interjections like "hum-hum." Of route, do now not abuse it. Sometimes it's miles hard to avoid monologues if someone is happy or is telling a tale, however make sure this does not show up often and simplest whilst important. Remember to use frame language and movements to supplement the communicate. In actual lifestyles, human beings frequently speak via nonverbal cues along with gestures, facial expressions, and posture. Including the ones statistics to your writing can help deliver your characters to existence and make their speak extra possible.

Another element that disrupts the narrative's tempo and diverts the reader is expository speech. It's a manner of using speak to carry important records the reader may otherwise not recognize.

Something that the aforementioned talk from City of Bones is also doing. In the scene, Jace is speakme to his colleagues and the demon, all of whom already recognize what a demon is. The purpose of the speech serves only to inform Clary, who is hiding, and the reader himself. It's a clumsy manner of revealing information because it prevents the reader or the characters from discovering it honestly via occasions in the story.

However, it's moreover something each author has accomplished in advance than, myself protected. You can use communicate to reveal information or proof to be able to growth the plot definitely, but if the characters are already aware of it, do now not repeat it in communicate sincerely to tell the reader.

The opposite can also result in an infodump alert. If a person is not privy to the statistics being shared by using using the character speakme, the writer looks like it is an outstanding possibility to tell the reader using speech. This results in a huge speech and masses of statistics being shared proper away, with a purpose to distract the reader and purpose them to become disinterested.

People do no longer talk as despite the fact that they have got ingested a textbook or like they'll be museum body of employees (until your man or woman is honestly a manual). Unfortunately, this mistake is likewise not unusual in novice writers. Just go to the first few pages of my first e-book:

"Diabolus Venator emerge as set up within the 12 months 1870". Diabolus Venator changed into a Latin call of the agency and meant Demon Hunter. It had been named at a time whilst Latin mottos and names have been even though in fashion, however I come to be nonetheless amazed with the useful resource of the literal this means that and absence of originality. Anya Marie regarded pretty inquisitive about what I changed into saying. I, however, regarded to be lower again at college giving a large oral presentation that have become going to be decisive in my final grade. "Created thru the use of Harrison Maxwell and Stephen Wilfred, who have been an proper instance of a muscle and thoughts duo. Maxwell come to be a military man within the army and Wilfred have emerge as a historian focusing on paranormal activities.

The nineteenth century changed into in which basically the entire data of the supernatural began out. Until then, humans had superstitions and beliefs about spirits and demons, however it wasn't until the start of that century that increasingly mediums began out performing, claiming to talk to ghosts. It changed into moreover some years earlier that human beings started having superstitions approximately vampires and protective themselves with crosses and garlic. Even although it have become all bullocks, but the horrible sods did no longer realize that.

www.ingramcontent.com/pod-product-compliance
Lightning Source LLC
Chambersburg PA
CBHW070734020526
44118CB00035B/1328